SACRED LANDSCAPE

By Bob Mander

 **New Generation Publishing**

ACKNOWLEDGEMENTS

I would like to acknowledge the tremendous debt of gratitude that I owe to Niven Sinclair for his constant interest, support and encouragement during my endeavours and for inviting us into his home in Surrey. Conversations with him are always interesting and informative. I would particularly wish to thank him for agreeing to write the Foreword for 'Sacred Landscape', particularly in view of his amazingly busy schedule.

Many thanks too to David Russell for agreeing to allow me to use some of his photographs and for his brief tutorial on dowsing to Avis and I at Chiswick House.

Many thanks to those friends and colleagues who have read the rough copy of the book and encouraged me to publish it, and to Avis for her company, constant encouragement and dowsing some of the sites with me.

I would like to thank Daniel Cooke of New Generation Publishing for his guidance and patience in bringing this book to publication.

Many people have agreed to allow me to use their photographs and/or illustrations, for which I am extremely grateful.

1)   John Glover for his photos of the shadows at Long Meg and Castlerigg stone circles and for his atmospheric photo of Swinside circle.

2)   Ian Farnworth of Maxima Systems I.T. Consultancy for all the photographs of the Isle of Man.

3)   Simon Lewis for the Cheesewring, Grimspound and Men-an tol photos.

4)   Margaret Curtis for Cailleach na Mointeach and Callanish 1.

5)   Stubob (Modern Antiquarian website) for the Woodhenge Cairn.*

6)   a23 (Modern Antiquarian website) for Cnoc Fillibhear Bheag.*

7)   Don Jacobsen for the resurgent spring at Malham Cove.

8)   David Wheatley of the Negotiating Avebury Project for the Beckhampton Stone.

9)   North Coastal Community Journal of North Norfolk for Seahenge.

10)   Simon Brighton for the photos of Royston Cave.

11)   Charles Tait for his photos of the Orkneys.

12)   Bath Tourism Plus for the photograph of the Roman Baths.

13)   Howard Pankhurst for the photograph of St. Nectan's Well

* I have attempted to contact Stubob and a23 through the website without success.

To -   Avis (now sadly passed on).
My companion on life's journey, for all her help and
encouragement and for being there.

And -   Rose
A wonderful friend and guide.

PREFACE

This book does not purport to just give an outline of the archaeology of the British Isles in Neolithic and Bronze Age times. It is in reality, an attempt to cut through the scholarly studies that have been published about the various locations mentioned in the text and to try to present an interpretation of the sites from a spiritual point of view. Archaeologists tend to eschew talk of the religion and spiritual philosophy of the ancients, citing the fact that with no written language there can be no definite information about those issues. They prefer to discuss the potential 'ritual' aspects of various features. Likewise the book does not claim to be completely up-to-date with the very latest research on prehistoric archaeology. The author has followed discoveries made in the past couple of years on topics as diverse as the Rotherwas Ribbon, the latest finds at Stonehenge, at Kilmartin Glen, around the Hill of Tara in Eire and the like and sees no reason to change his interpretation of the religious philosophy of our forebears on these islands.

However, I do believe that there are significant pointers to these beliefs that can be adumbrated from the nature of the sites, the place names relating to many of the locations etc.. I likewise believe that the belief systems of Neolithic man in Britain and Ireland reflect a fairly sophisticated philosophy - one that has been lost in the materialism in the world in which we live nowadays. It is true to say that many people in our modern society are starting to question the religion with which they have been fed for the past couple of thousand years and to seek new answers (or even ancient answers!) to the problems that beset us. I believe that the concepts espoused by the ancients bear a direct relevance to our modern life. A return to a more compassionate, caring, feminine approach as a counterbalance to the more aggressive male tendencies can only be of benefit to modern society. Their beliefs on life and death, the importance of nature and the use of earth energies would seem to give messages for modern living.

Bob Mander (August, 2013)

Contents

FOREWORD

Ever since Bob asked me to write a Foreword for his book, I have written thousands of words. All of them inadequate. All of them binned. There are times when words, for all their powerful meaning, are only pale shadows of the things they purport to convey. This has been one of those occasions. There aren't enough superlatives for me to be able to describe the impact which this amazing book has made made on me. It may not have changed my life but it has changed my thinking. When I walk my dog, I no longer take a single step without thinking of the 'Sacred Landscape' beneath my feet.

"Sacred Landscape"? What thoughts do these words evoke? I immediately think of Mother Earth from whom all bounty flows - whether it be the food we eat or the clothes we wear, whether it be the house we live in or the car we drive. Bob's book tells us the history of the sacred sites which abound in this Emerald Isle of ours; of the goddesses which were to be found exercising benign influences over people and places; of lines of energy which run across these islands; of hills and forts; of caves and graves; of monoliths and stone circles; of green men and holy wells. The list goes on and on until one feels that there is no part of our native land which is without some sacred link. And so it is because Mother Earth nourishes our spirit as well as our bodies. She provides her own altars for us to worship at - altars which all to often have been hi-jacked by the Church and been desecrated in the process. If there has been any sacrilege it is what Man has done to

Mother Earth - to our sacred landscape.

When I was in Africa and saw the wholesale loss of land through water or wind erosion, I would tell the Africans that their only wealth was the land under their feet; that the tree was their brother; that the forest was their friend. Destroy them at their peril. The same message applies here where concrete and tarmac are preventing our natural link - our umbilical link with Mother Earth. We also sever that at our peril.

The "Sacred Landscape" should be in every library. It should be in every school because it tells us more about our island home than all the geography and history books combined. It is a monumental work. It does not tell us to be green but it does tell us to be aware of and respect the "Sacred Landscape" we are privileged to live in.

I have been enriched (beyond measure) by reading Bob's book. You will be too. That I can safely guarantee. I get a simple pleasure by just holding the book.

Niven Sinclair (August,2013).

STONEHENGE DAWN

A study of the ancient sites of Britain and Eire, produced by our forebears. What is it that makes them sacred? What is their relevance for the modern age?

Thanks are due again in full measure to our friends locally and beyond! Many thanks to John Glover and David Russell for permission to use their photographs and for Niven Sinclair for his help and encouragement.

1. Introduction and Forethoughts

It is the intention in this book to look at the landscape of Britain and Ireland, with its numerous sacred elements and to attempt to evaluate the evolution of the landscape in those terms and to endeavour to highlight elements of the spirituality that seems to be inherent in the land in which we live.

Is it possible to trace a continuous strain of sacredness in our landscape from prehistoric times through to the present day? Are there spiritual lessons that were understood by our distant (some would say primitive!) ancestors that are but dimly recognised by the vast majority of people nowadays? Who are the people that have attempted to preserve such knowledge from ancient times?

In order to endeavour to answer these questions and others, it is proposed to study many of the ancient, sacred sites that abound in these 'Islands of Light' - stone circles, megaliths, barrows, chambered cairns and sites of natural sanctity recognised by our early ancestors, such as tors, rock outcrops, wells and springs. Some locations have retained their sanctity with more recent usage and these will be looked at too.

There are undoubtedly sacred complexes around the British Isles that have remained steeped in spirituality for thousands of years. Is it possible to detect what it is that makes them sacred and why they have remained so over the centuries? One has only to think of the Avebury area in Wiltshire, the Kilmartin Glen region of Argyll, the area around Arbor low in Derbyshire and the Bruna Boinne area of Eire to realise that some parts of the land have a special spiritual significance.

As a starting point for a study of our sacred landscape, three quotations have been selected from the works of two authors who are steeped in a spiritual approach to the consideration of the concept of what 'sacred' means in terms of our landscape - namely Paul Devereux and John Michell. In numerous books over the years, they have examined the very essence of the sacred landscape. The forethoughts for this book, as drawn from their books, are appended below and provide a starting point for our consideration of 'Sacred Landscape'.

Forethoughts

1. "A sacred place can be as small as a tiny mound of stones or a single standing stone or as broad as the eye can see - a whole mountain range perhaps. 'Sacred place' could be said to operate at any scale, from a specific site, to a localised place, a scene or a whole landscape." (Devereux, 2000, pp. 24 - 25.)

2. "People felt secure in their own country, a sacred landscape inhabited by familiar spirits, each of which was visited in the course of the annual pilgrimage. Though it has left scarcely any physical mark upon the landscape, that way of life laid the foundations of native culture, which rest in the sacred places of the country. Certain spots, where the old British nomads gathered at the shrine of some nature spirit, are now marked by cathedrals and churches. Many have retained sacred and legendary associations from the old times." (Michell, 1996, p.5.)

3. "A sentiment which frequently occurs, particularly it seems, to English poets and mystics, alludes to some intangible mystery concealed within the landscape, an aesthetic law which ever defies formation. Some have attempted to define this law in poetry, others in science and philosophy. Yet we still do not know why it is that certain spots on the earth's surface are by general agreement more inspiring than others or how it happens that these very places so often coincide with the centres of prehistoric sanctity." (Michell, 1983, pp. 13 - 14.)
In the final quotation above, John Michell alludes to the inspiration that the sacred landscape can engender in

16

poets and mystics, amongst other persons attuned to the vibrations of the landscape. Three such interpretations can be studied in the following section which outline both the nature of our scenery and the problems that have developed as a result of modern man's interference.

2. The Vision

1. "And did those feet in ancient time Walk upon England's mountains green? And was the Holy Lamb of God
    On England's pleasant pastures seen?" (Blake - 'The Land of Dreams')

2. "There was a time when meadow, grove and stream, The earth and every common sight,
    To me did seem Apparelled in celestial light,
    The glory and freshness of a dream. It is not now as it hath been of yore - Turn wheresoe'er I may,
    By night or day,
        The things which I have seen I now can see no more.

        (Wordsworth - Ode - 'Intimations of Immortality.')

Blake was, of course, the great mystical poet, hymn writer and artist.
    Wordsworth was England's premier poet of nature and its links to the spiritual heart of the countryside.

Section One
The Stones Cry Out

Chapter One
Sacredness - Defining the Parameters

"sacred/ adj.1. Dedicated or set apart for the service or worship of a god or gods; 2a. Worthy of religious veneration, b. commanding reference or respect; 3. Of religion, not secular or profane.

> Longman's Concise English Dictionary, 1985,
> Merriam-Webster Inc.

It is proposed that this book will look at the nature of sacred sites in Britain and Ireland with reference to a number of examples. The idea of 'sacredness' will be based on the definitions 1, 2a and 2b in the dictionary reference above, viz. 'set apart for the service and worship of god or gods', 'worthy of religious veneration', and 'commanding reverence or respect'.

However it is impossible to progress further without gaining a clear understanding of what we mean by the term 'a sacred site'. How are they selected? What is it that makes them sacred? Devereux (2000) writes about 'sacred places' and feels that they have come about as a result of the interaction of two factors, namely some aspect of the geography of the site, such a prominent hill, combined with the minds of the people that conceive the site to be sacred. "The sacred place is neither mind nor locality but the sum of both." (Devereux,2000, p.11).

It is an interesting thought that, as one travels around the countryside, these ancient sites, which were imbued with sacredness often in Neolithic times, still have the power to induce the same feeling of awe and wonder in many modern observers. One can see many people lost in contemplation in these places, apparently undergoing some form of spiritual experience. The sense of power at such a site can only be put down to the '*genius loci*' or 'spirit of the place' - present for thousands of years and, although often diminished by lack of use, still available to the modern seeker.

It would appear that some aspect of the geography of the site must entail something rather more than the location on the top of the hill, or by a spring or such like. There must have been something rather more to the concept of sacredness than just a perception in people's minds, there must have also been a certain quality that imparts a sense of the sacred to it. We know that the ancients worshipped certain physical features of the landscape, perhaps in the form of a shape resembling a pregnant woman, lying on her back or a pair of breasts. This would probably be due to the emphasis on fertility in their rituals and a heartfelt reverence for the sacred feminine. However such an obvious cannot be ascribed to a host of other sites, so there must be some other factor involved.

It is the purpose of this book to examine whence the feeling of the sacred is derived, these 'magical places' as the spirit guide White Eagle has called them. We will examine many ancient sites, some re-used for later Christian worship, some not, and attempt to analyse the factors that brought about their initial use for worship, reverence and respect, thereby giving rise to the feeling of sacredness in them. More importantly, it is proposed to examine why it might be that this aura has survived into modern times and, if so, does it bear any relevance for the new millennium?

How is Sacredness Achieved?

There seems to be three possibilities as to how and why a site becomes sacred. There may be something about the site that defines it as 'sacred'

In the minds of the people and therefore they venerate it as such, perhaps much later building a stone circle or church there. Secondly, it could perhaps be that a site may actually acquire sacredness through usage and recognition by the people. Thirdly, it might possible be that a site is designated as sacred through the simple expedient of having a religious edifice erected upon it. In the context of this book, the latter option is fairly easily dispensed with - most people who enter a modern church building on a 'non-sacred' site will sense the lack of that 'special' atmosphere, notwithstanding that the ritual that takes place there may have a sacred purpose in the eyes of the congregation.

There can be no doubt at all that the first option, namely that the site has about it some inherent quality of the sacred is by far the most potent of the three. There can be no doubt too that the great majority of places selected by ancient peoples for their religious ceremonies had a particular quality that attracted them in the first place - this point will be considered in greater detail in the next four chapters. Is it perhaps that that there was something about the site in relation to the sun and moon at particular times of the year, or was it something about the energies to be found there that the people, or at least their shaman/priests sensed?

It may well be too that certain sites may, in fact acquire a feeling of spirituality through the nature of their usage and the nature of the user over a period of time. Such a place may well be the old Templar church and Commandery at Balantradoch (now Temple) in Midlothian, Scotland. This is a site that exudes a feeling of the sacred, plus, nowadays, a distinct aura of sadness.

Devereux (2000) postulates no less than eleven roles that may be fulfilled by sacred places, he summarised them as follows (p.40) :-

They - represented a mythic or spiritual presence in the landscape;

-   marked where spirits or deities dwelled;

-   were where a sense of the numinous (awe-inspiring) was provoked;

-   were for the worship of supernatural powers and other spiritual and ritual activity

-   memorialised a historic, mythic or otherwise important event;

-   were for burial, the placing of ancestors in the landscape;

- created a funerary geography for ritual and ceremony;

- mapped an otherworld geography;

- were for consulting the gods;

- represented a cosmological feature;

-   linked heaven and earth by means of

22

astronomical orientation, for ceremonial purposes based on astrological or cosmological principles.

It is quite clear that these roles relate to a wide range of sites that can be classed as sacred, from barrows, dolmens and monoliths all the way up to the magnificent stone circles.

The truly significant point about many of the items on the above list is that they demonstrate that heaven and earth were closely linked in the minds of the ancients - usually summarised as 'as above, so below'. We will take a closer look at this significant theme in the following chapters.

Chapter Two
Spirits of Hills, Woods and Streams

The following chart shows the time periods associated with the ancient peoples of Britain and Ireland.

→ 4700 B.C.E. - Mesolithic.

4700 - 4300 B.C.E. - Very Early Neolithic. 4300 - 3500 B.C.E. - Early Neolithic.

3500 - 3200 B.C.E. - Middle Neolithic. 3200 - 2000 B.C.E. - Late Neolithic.

2000 - 500 B.C.E. - Bronze Age.

500 B.C.E. → -Iron Age.

The Mesolithic and the Early Neolithic periods might be described as a sort of 'Golden Age' in spiritual terms - man and nature existed in a largely harmonious relationship because man respected natural law and did not attempt to divert it from its set course - balance was all important.

As Michell (1996) states (p.5) :-

"People felt secure in their own country, a sacred landscape inhabited by familiar spirits, each of which was visited in the course of the annual pilgrimage. Though it has left hardly any physical mark upon the landscape, that way of life laid the foundations of native culture, which rests in the sacred places of the country. Certain spots, where the old British nomads gathered at the shrine of some nature spirit, are now marked by cathedrals and churches.

Many have retained sacred and legendary associations from the old times."

It should be remembered that, at this time, the population was gathered in family groups and often a number of such families travelled together.

The landscape at this time comprised deciduous woodland. The coniferous woods that immediately followed the last Ice Age, roughly twelve thousand years ago, had gradually been pushed northwards under the influence of the warmer climate and heavier rainfall. England comprised mainly oak woodland, with hazel, alder, elm, elder and lime mixed in, in varying proportions depending on the nature of the soil. Birch was found in the more acidic soils of Devon, Cornwall and much of Wales.

Clearing in Deciduous Woodland Near St. Bega's Church, Cumbria

It is within this wooded landscape that we must picture the native people of the countryside living. They were nomadic hunter-gatherers who developed their own territory and travelled around it in the course of the year. Regular campsites were established, often by springs or a suitable river crossing. Another likely site might be a clearing in the forest (as above). Their annual route around their land was navigated by sighting on prominent hills, streams and perhaps with the aid of the stars.

It follows that the regular stopping places on the annual pilgrimage of the group acquired 'sacredness' and were to be welcomed as a sanctified place by the group. Eventually, these sites were given their own 'spirit of the place' to watch over them and the group. Such places might be caves, springs or clearings in the forest - the latter to eventually become the sacred places of the Druids, the priests of the Celtic tribes (such an example is pictured above).

As the pattern evolved, so the major landmarks and stopping places acquired their own *'genius loci'* and usually had their own nature spirits assigned to them. These spirits were, more often than not, feminine. The religion, such as it might be called, was concerned with fertility - birth, death and rebirth, of the people and the land. Animals were killed purely for food and gratitude would always have been expressed to the benevolent spirits for providing the prey. Similarly the nuts and fruits of the forest were seen as part of nature's bounty and the continuing survival of the group depended upon the continuity of the animal species and the new growth of the vegetation in the following spring.

It follows that the physical features of the landscape are often worshipped if they happened to resemble, for instance, a pregnant woman lying on her back or a pair of female breasts. Man knew that his continued existence depended on his relationship with, and the benevolence of, nature. Our ancient ancestors also, on occasion, by the efforts of the group made small modifications to the landscape to protect the appearance of a feature of the landscape. An example of this can be observed at the Cheesewring in Cornwall (see following page).Occasionally man would assist nature by carving or shaping features to more resemble the object of worship. The stress laid on fertility is further emphasised by the carved figurines that have been discovered all over Britain and Europe in the shape of what are obvious fertility goddesses. An excellent example is to be seen in the figurine from Grimes Graves in Norfolk, this is a group of some four hundred pits from which flints were mined (see page 13).

The spiritual emphasis at this time then was on the feminine aspect of life, with a variety of Goddess figures worshipped at caves, trees or woods and springs. Perhaps the main goddess in Britain was Bridgit, goddess of fire, also known as the swan goddess. In Dorset there are two rivers - Brit and Bride, on which stands the town of Bridport. Near the mouths of the rivers stands the Abbotsbury Swannery, home to hundreds of swans every year. Derivatives of her name are found all over Britain, including the name Britain itself and the figure found on coins, namely Britannia.

Mam Tor, Derbyshire

The Cheesewring, Bodmin Moor, Cornwall

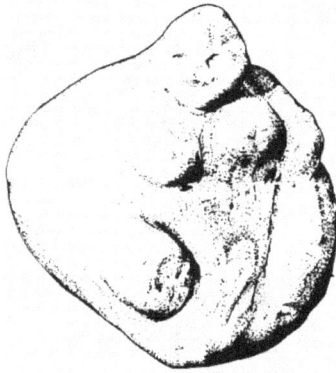

Grimes Graves Goddess

Considering the fertility aspect of her role, the word 'bride' is also a derivation. She gradually evolved from the Goddess of Fire into the caring, compassionate Universal Goddess. In Ireland, she became Brid and was associated with fertility and midwifery. Healing was another important element of the deity. As happens in all religions the Celts and their Druid priests eventually formalised the worship of Bridget somewhat and she duly took her place in the Celtic calendar at the festival of Imbolg, February 1st. This date is, significantly, related to her main role for it heralded the onset of spring and the gradual lengthening of the days. Needless to say, the Christians later sanctified her as St. Bridget in an attempt to eliminate the association with the old 'pagan' religion of the ancients. The first of February became Candlemas in the Christian calendar - a festival of light. Her name still occurs in many parts of Britain and Ireland, in rivers and place names. To the ancient Welsh, England was known as Prydain (Britain) and significantly the Priddy henges are still to be found south of Bristol. The Brigantes, the tribe that inhabited northern England in pre-Roman times, were dedicated to the worship of Bridget, Brid or Brig.

Other goddesses were to be found exercising a significant influence on the native peoples of Britain. Koeur was at the heart of all living things and her name can be recognised in the modern French word for heart, *coeur,* and also in words such as 'core', 'corn' and 'kernel'. It may also be recognised in the word 'acre' as a measure of land. She also gave her name to trees such as the sycamore and the oak (acorn). She also became the goddess of the hills and many words associated with her worship are still to be found in English, Welsh and Scottish - 'cairn', 'carn', 'caer', 'cader' and the Scandinavian word 'scar', found in many parts of northern England as a word for a rock outcrop. Other names ascribed to the goddess are Keridwen and Cernunno, the latter eventually to become a male god, similar in aspect to Herne the Hunter.

The goddess Ma needs little introduction as the figure of motherhood. She also became the goddess of truth. Words derived from her name are fairly obvious, including 'mother' ('mater' in Latin, 'mere' in French), 'mate' and 'mattress'. She was also 'madron' ('matron'), - "mother of all, bounteous water of life". Her name is still to be found in the British landscape as at Marden Henge and Mam Tor in Derbyshire (see page 12), a sacred hill shaped like a woman's breast (mammary). She was also the goddess of sacred places such as natural wells and springs. The ancient Starwell Spring at Biddestone in Wiltshire is one such of these places - a water source for the travelling people and visited by them for centuries.

The Starwell Holy Well, Wiltshire.

The river Derwent in Derbyshire rises in a series of springs and flows through the spa town of Matlock Bath. The goddess Hueur was the spirit of the family and hence words such as 'home', 'hearth', 'hostel' and even 'hovel' are derived from her name.

She was also associated with agriculture and we still have words such as 'herdsman' and 'hoe' based on her name. Her name is still commemorated in place names such as Hawarden in North Wales, Crickhowell in South Wales, Haworth in Yorkshire and the Knap of Howar in the Orkneys. She was the origin of the word 'holy' in that her name meant 'Great Hole'.

The goddess Ver was seen as the goddess of fire

and water, the fire aspect is reflected in words such as 'furnace', 'forge' and 'fire' itself. The water aspect shows from the old word 'a'vern' which became 'afon' in Welsh, Avon and the word 'river' itself. All river mouths in Wales are referred to as 'aber' and hence town names such as Aberavon or Aberystwyth. Her name is also reflected in 'ferry', 'ford' and the Scandinavian word 'force' or 'foss' as a term for a waterfall in Northern England.

Probably the mother goddess of all these was Ur, the archetypal goddess of Western Europe and the Middle East. She may be perceived as the originator of the goddess cult and her name is linked with Astarte, Asherah and Isis - the great goddesses of the Middle East. She was the goddess of the Universe - to the Scandivavians she was Vod or Urtha, from which derive the word 'earth'. The name for Ireland, Eire, is likewise a derivation of her name, as is the language of that country, Erse.

With the onset of the Age of Taurus, the gentle Neolithic Age gave way to the Bronze and then the Iron Ages, when people tended to settle in one place more than they had previously and weapons developed. A more aggressive society was developing, one that was increasingly male orientated and patriarchal. This process was speeded up by the arrival of the Romans and then eventually the aggressively patriarchal Christian church - not its somewhat gentler Celtic predecessor. The place of woman was progressively downgraded and the worship of the Goddess (in whichever form) to a large extent disappeared.

We have already seen how the Church tried to 'lose' the 'pagan' Bridgit or Bridget by making her into a saint and changing her background. The story of assimilation or destruction continues. Ma became the faerie queen Mab - a sprite of the woods and meadows. The word 'smatter' became a word for a gossipy old woman. Hueur was denigrated as the word 'whore', in fact in some parts this latter word is still pronounced like the name of the goddess. Koeur became used in such words as 'cure' and 'accursed'. As we have already stated, she lost her femininity when being changed into the male god, Cernunno. Ver gave rise to words such as 'aver' and 'aversion', and Ur produced words like 'err', 'erase', 'irritate' and 'irrational'. It is amazing what introducing a negative element into words can do and how subtle psychological warfare can be!

The goddesses listed above were also envisaged by the people in their triple aspect, that is they were perceived by the people as reflecting all the aspects of womanhood, namely as maiden, mother and old woman (also called the crone or hag). In these three guises they showed the development from physical beauty through womanhood to wrinkled old age, but, at the same time, the growth from spiritual innocence through to a mature knowledge. An old woman was usually the wise woman or shaman of the family group, reflecting the status of the goddess.

It is significant that the ancient people went to considerable trouble to identify sacred landscapes which resembled a recumbent female form - usually a range of hills with suitable intervening valleys. This would also entail an appropriate viewing place being selected to worship the outline. These places were usually said to represent the crone or hag. Examples of such include Cailleach na Mointeach (The Old Woman of the Moors) near Callanish, Cnoc Cailliche

33

(Hill of the Hag) in Aberdeenshire and Hag Hill on the Michael Line. Mam Tor has already been mentioned.

Cailleach na Mointeach

In the early Jewish religion, particularly as viewed by the gnostics, women played a far more prominent role than in immediate pre-Christian times. Jehovah had two wives, who might be equated to Hoeur (see above), denoted by the Jewish name of HWH. As they were sidelined in the later aspects of the religion, the name became JHWH of Jahweh, which simply referred to their male god, Jehovah.

The Christian church dealt with this triple goddess differently by ultimately converting them into the Father, Son and Holy Spirit!

In the ancients' worship of trees and springs, we can detect evidence of the veneration of fertility and the

34

cycle of life, death and rebirth - all of these important to the physical survival and spiritual wellbeing of the people. Living as they did in deciduous woodland, they could see that the trees seemed to die in the autumn, remaining so through the winter months, only for the signs of rebirth in the spring and the growth to maturity in the summer months. Small wonder then that the ancients eventually devised special days to commemorate these clearly defined aspects of the natural cycle. These were later formalised by the Celts (Kelts) and their Druid priesthood. This is outlined in the following simple diagram, based on the circled or Celtic cross.

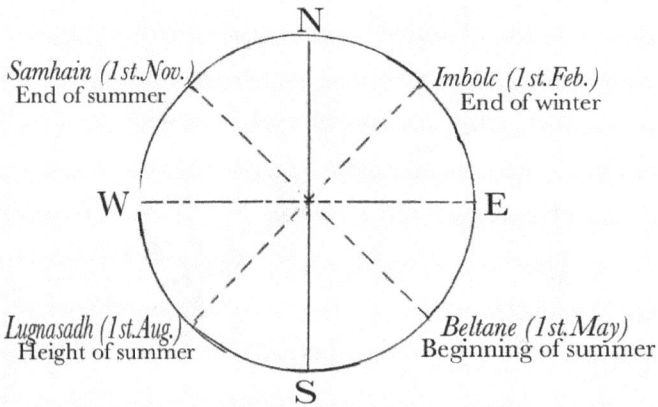

THE CELTIC YEAR

As Juliette Wood (2000, page 25.) states :-

"The Celtic year has no beginning and no end, but follows the rhythms of nature in a continuous cycle. The markers on the calendar are the changes evident in nature. Each new season has a festival that celebrates its agricultural significance. During these festivities, the boundaries between the material and supernatural worlds are dissolved, and the ghostly inhabitants of the Otherworld break through to enter the realm of the living."

In the above diagram, the centre of the circle is marked by the Tree of life.

As Yvonne Abuurow (1993, p.9) states:-

"The tree represents the whole of manifestation, the synthesis of earth and water, and dynamic life. It is both imago mundi and axis mundi, joining the three worlds (heaven, earth and underworld) and making communication between them possible. It gives access to the power of the sun; it is also an omphalos, a centre of dragon energy or etheric power. It is the feminine principle, nourishing, sheltering and protecting; trees are often depicted as female figures. As world axis it is linked to the mountain and the pillar."

This tree in later times became the Maypole around which revellers danced to celebrate the onset of spring. We will discuss the significance of dancing around in this fashion in a later chapter. It is interesting to note that Beltane is still to some extent celebrated as May Day, although in Celtic times it was somewhat of a 'moveable feast', depending as it did on the appearance of the first 'may' blossom on the hawthorn bushes.

Springs were also of great significance to the so-called 'pagans' - the waters rose in what was perceived as the Underworld (or Otherworld), the darkness beneath, and coming into the light of day to provide nourishment. This too was seen as symbolic as a rebirth from death. The Underworld was the realm of Cernunno (Herne the Hunter, the horned god of nature and it was he who sent the water to nourish the vegetation and the animals, as well as the human population.

In summary then, the people throughout most of the Neolithic times lived a nomadic lifestyle within their own group territories.

Unsurprisingly they grew to reverence certain obvious landmarks on their annual route - perhaps a cave used to shelter the family in winter, a spring where they could camp and be sure of water, a clearing in the woodland or a rocky outcrop or hill that they could use as their line of sight on the march. Eventually these landmarks were given 'protectresses' in the form of goddesses or 'spirits of the site' and these were worshipped by the group. Michell (1996,p.6) has gone as far as to suggest :-

"An elderly person may sometimes have been left by the travelling group to shelter by a sacred spring, later to become its resident priest, priestess or oracle."

Sometimes a prominent feature such as a hill bore an uncanny resemblance to their goddess and was worshipped as such. Thus were the first elements of our sacred landscape 'laid out' on the ground, to be built on by future generations.

As the goddess concept developed and the idea of the triple aspect of the goddess became implanted in the mind of the ancient people - perhaps as a recognition of the maturation process in humans - with the innocent, 'unworldly' maiden, then the mother and, finally the worldly-wise old crone or hag, with her vast store of wisdom about nature and the weather, so the identification with the landscape developed. The ancients looked to the distance and identified landscape features that they could reverence as similitudes of their goddess. Increasingly, throughout the Neolithic period, people were starting to settle down in these familiar places, sacred to them and new concepts of worship within this landscape were developing.

Chapter Three
Spirits of Earth and Sky "As above, so below."

As the Neolithic period progressed, so the nomadic family groups of our ancient forebears gradually adopted a more settled existence. Although there has been some evidence recently from Northumberland that some settlements were built during the Mesolithic, it has not been proved that they were either numerous or used all year round. The settlements constructed in the Neolithic age reflected the move towards agriculture rather than hunting or gathering. Groups started to keep animals and grow crops such as oats and wheat. Of necessity, this involved a radical change from their previous mode of existence.

Settlements tended to be located on the chalk hills of southern Britain and on the high moors elsewhere, bearing in mind that the climate at this time was wamer and wetter than it has been in the last thousand years. The move to higher land avoided the necessity for woodland clearance which would have been needed in the clay lowlands. Accordingly small hamlets developed such as Grimspound on Dartmoor, which dates from perhaps 1000 B.C.E. (see picture on the following page). The site was enclosed by a wall three metres thick and two metres high. Within the enclosure were about twenty seven hut circles and cattle pens. The cattle and sheep would have been penned in at night to protect them from wild animals and allowed to graze on the nearby moorland by day. The compound was serviced by its own stream and therefore could be self sufficient in times of necessity.

As the Bronze Age advanced, so the pattern became more complex and field systems enclosed by dry stone walling, collected from the surface of the granitic moorland, evolved as can be seen from the accompanying map of Zennor parish in west Cornwall, taken from W.G.Hoskins excellent book - 'The Making of the English Landscape.' Because of their nature, these stone walls are still in existence today, some two and a half thousand years later.

Grimspound Settlement on Dartmoor

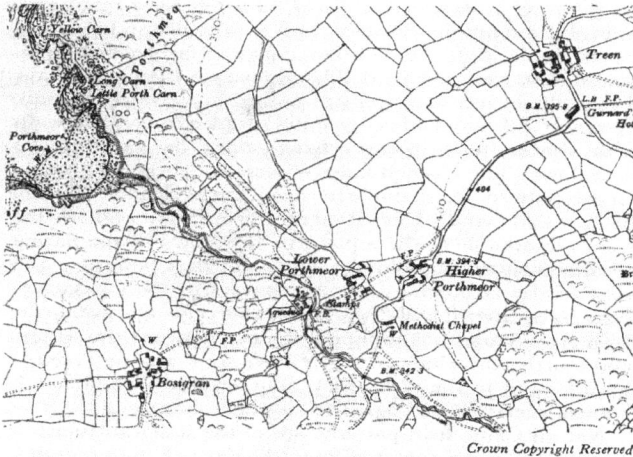

Celtic Fields in Zennor Parish

This change to a pastoral/agricultural lifestyle clearly had a profound effect on the style of worship of the population. No longer was it practicable to move around the hallowed landscape worshipping at the old shrines. Instead, special places were created by the people where the old goddesses would be venerated. These sites were, as often as not, placed in some proximity to previous sacred sites such as hills or rocky outcrops - an obvious attempt to maintain continuity. Examples of such places will be studied in greater depth later in the chapter.

Monuments have been discovered constructed of wood and others of stone. It would appear likely that wood was originally used as the construction medium although, as the wood has long since rotted away, very little actual evidence has been discovered. Post holes have been identified where the wood has rotted away and the former holes have been filled with soil of a different colour to the surroundings. These have taken the form of single

41

post holes, possibly resulting from the Neolithic equivalent of a totem pole, or circles of post holes - Stonehenge was originally a timber circle approached by an avenue comprising parallel lines of timber posts.

It is quite possible that single wooden posts were carved with totemic animals such as the bear, the wolf or the deer, as a focus for tribal worship - much in the same manner as the native American Indians did until comparatively recently. Indeed the tribal shamen also wore masks of the particular animals they were associated with, their protectors in the spirit world in which they wandered. The shaman was thought to be the tribal oracle, producing words of wisdom and advice to help in the hunt or to warn of danger. Much of this wisdom was acquired and delivered in a trance state, produced under the influence of hallucinogenic drugs such as magic mushrooms, or from the slightly radio-active and therefore trance inducing water from certain springs (Devereux, 1995).

Shaman

42

It has recently been announced that a ring of postholes, supposedly the remnants of a group of totem poles, has been discovered at Kilmartin Glen in Argyllshire, Scotland. The magazine 'British Archaeology' announced in Issue 64, April, 2002 :-
"An early Bronze Age timber circle containing an inner ring of totem poles set around a deep, sacred pool is thought to have once stood at the head of the Kilmartin Valley in Argyll, site of one of Scotland's richest concentrations of prehistoric ritual monuments." Kilmartin Glen will be discussed in greater detail in a later chapter.

It is now believed by some authorities that the famous cave paintings of sacred sites such as Lascaux in central France and the carved symbols found on megaliths in many parts of Britain and Ireland were produced under the influence of the same hallucinogenic trance states. Cave paintings have not been found in Britain, save for one poor example in a cave in the Midlands, but the numerous abstract rock symbols, which obviously carried some meaning to the people of the time, do show quite an advanced thinking. The stalactites, stalagmites and pillars found in limestone caves were often considered to be sacred by the hunter-gatherers, with animal likenesses ascribed to them - much as the guides showing people around such caves do nowadays! Symbols are discussed in greater detail in Chapter 10.

Sketch of Long Meg Standing Stone, showing symbols

There are two good examples of sacred sites constructed of timber - one from preserved timbers at the location now known as Seahenge on the Norfolk coast and one where circles of postholes have been discovered and replaced by concrete pillars at Woodhenge, near Stonehenge in Wiltshire.

Seahenge

Seahenge, so-called because it was discovered on a Norfolk beach where the sea has been eroding layers of peat, was a circle of 55 oak posts with a tree in the centre. It has been carbon dated to the year 2000 B.C.E.

The timber is all of oak wood, sacred to the ancients. The central tree had fallen, or been felled, prior to being placed in the circle and had been located in the centre of the circle in an upside-down position, i.e. with its roots in the air. All the timbers showed signs of having been shaped with hand tools.

Yvonne Aburrow (1993, p.10) has this to say about trees placed upside down :-

"The inverted tree is a magical tree; the roots in the air and the branches in the earth represented inverted action, that which is on high descending below and that which is below ascending on high. It is the principle of 'as above, so below', the reflection of the celestial and terrestrial worlds in each other." We will return to this concept shortly.

Woodhenge was of a different form altogether from Seahenge in that it was erected in a series of near-concentric circles with a small kist containing a child's skeleton very close to the central point. Whilst Castleden has postulated that this was once a thatched roundhouse similar to those that must have been found in the neighbouring Durrington Walls, which have been construed by some as a sort of 'university' or lodging for pilgrims visiting the many ritual sites centred on Stonehenge itself, it must be said that Woodhenge has the 'feel' of a sacred site with a ritual purpose. The sheer volume of postholes would seem to preclude the likelihood of it being a

45

roundhouse, particularly combined with the child burial, possibly ritual.

Woodhenge

The atmosphere of the place seems also to indicate that it was something rather special. The dowsed energies at the site are clear, linking up the posts in the circle, in spite of them being concrete replacements for timber. The long axis of the site points towards the entrance to the henge and the whole is orientated towards the rise of the midsummer sun (see Chapter 4).

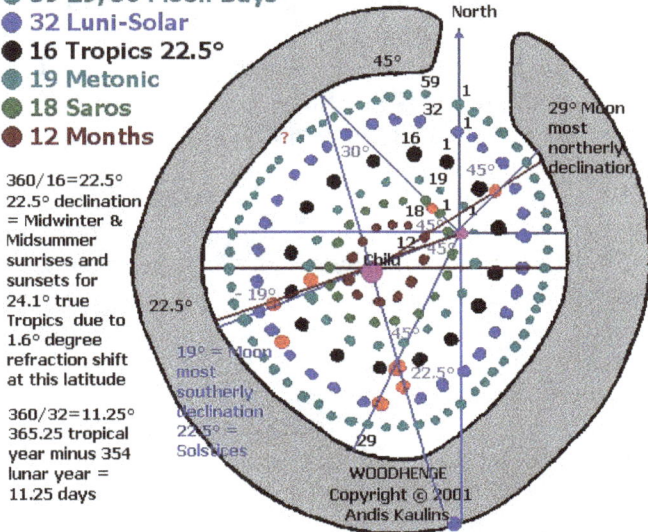

WOODHENGE

- So-called "extra" holes or stones
- 59 29/30 Moon Days
- 32 Luni-Solar
- 16 Tropics 22.5°
- 19 Metonic
- 18 Saros
- 12 Months

North

45°
59
32
16
19
18
12
Child
30°
19°
19° = Moon most southerly declination
22.5° = Solstices
29
45°
45°
45°
45°
22.5°
22.5°
1
1
1
?

29° Moon most northerly declination

360/16=22.5°
22.5° declination
= Midwinter &
Midsummer
sunrises and
sunsets for
24.1° true
Tropics due to
1.6° degree
refraction shift
at this latitude

360/32=11.25°
365.25 tropical
year minus 354
lunar year =
11.25 days

WOODHENGE
Copyright © 2001
Andis Kaulins

Woodhenge post and stone positions based on a drawing of Woodhenge at p. 68 of Astronomie in Stein [Astronomy in Stone] by Rudolf Drößler, Panorama Verlag, Wiesbaden, Germany, ISBN 3-926642-25-4. This is NOT a surveyed grid. All lines, numbers, labels, colors, degrees and decipherment added by Andis Kaulins. Graph may be reproduced as long as Copyright notice retained.

It seems that, at some stage, our forebears decided that wood was not sufficiently durable for their sacred monuments and, despite the tremendous extra work involved, started to erect stone circles and megaliths for the worship of their gods.

To return to the concept of 'as above, so below' mentioned earlier in relation to Seahenge, it may be remembered that this phrase is the generally recognised summary from the works of the great philosopher/ magician Hermes Trismegistus (thrice majestic), which he caused to be inscribed on his 'Emerald Tablet'

An extract from the Tablet reads :-
"What is below is like that which is above, and what is

47

above is similar to that which is below to accomplish the wonders of one thing. As all things were produced by the mediation from one being, so all things were produced from this one by adaptation. Its father is the sun; its mother is the moon. It is the cause of all perfection throughout the earth. Its power is perfect if it is changed into earth."

So it seems that our so-called 'primitive' ancestors had a clear spiritual view of the association between 'heaven' or the heavens and the earth on which they lived. It is clear that the standing stones (monoliths) and stone circles and their timber predecessors were directing the attention of the populace upwards towards the source of their being - be that the sun or the Great Spirit, which furnished them with the clouds and rain, and the warmth that fed them, their animals and their crops - in other words the natural law that governed their lives.

It is clear that the ancients took seriously the construction of 'heaven on earth' and there does seem to be a body of evidence to support the view that the sudden explosion in the numbers of monuments that clearly link heaven and earth, all over the world, must have come from some central location in the first place - such as Plato's Atlantis. Thus we find a similar blooming of monuments, often of a very similar design, based on observations of the stars and the planets, in such wide ranging parts of the world as Central America, Britain, the Canary Islands, Egypt and the Far East. It is well worthy of note that this building programme, which commenced in the Age of Taurus, six thousand years ago, and then to some extent in the Age of Aries, has been carried on in the face of huge odds in the Piscean Age by the Celtic Church, the Templars, the Cathars and the Rosicrucians amongst others. It is also noteworthy that one of the last truly great buildings that seem to reflect 'as above, so below' was St. Paul's Cathedral, designed by Sir Christopher Wren - a noted Rosicrucian and member of the 'Invisible College' who also supervised the construction. The cathedral was built on the site of a succession of sacred buildings stretching back to pre-Christian times. It should be remembered that, against all the odds, St. Paul's 'miraculously' survived the Great Blitz of London during the Second World War when all the surrounding buildings were destroyed. It is worthy of comment that, despite the vicissitudes of war, the great gothic cathedrals of France, constructed by the Knights Templar, also survived largely unscathed.

St. Paul's Cathedral, 1940

So, during the middle and late Neolithic times, our ancestors started to erect the great henges, stone circles, burial mounds and monoliths that testify to their belief in the cycle of nature, birth, death and reincarnation. Great indeed must have been their faith to have so persevered with these great cathedrals and churches of the Neolithic! Castleden (1990, p.100) clearly realised that the stone circles at least represented an important symbolic and spiritual feature to the tribal shamen :- "….. the circular or near circular form chosen for nearly all the enclosures was certainly symbolic. The circle represented the sun on whose warmth everything depended, but it also represented the world-disc; the banks simulating the far horizon bounding the world of men and the enclosed temenos (territory) a microcosm of the world itself

This microcosm was fully within the priest-magician's power to control; he could gather and focus beneficent forces there; he could, conversely, send the gathered forces out like the fertilising rays of the sun itself into the surrounding fields, meadows and forests, calling the larger world into fruitful submission."

So what of the old goddesses of the wandering groups? It may be said that the advent of fixed monuments did not mark the end of triple goddess worship in the middle and late Neolithic. Settings of three standing stones, often set within the perimeter of a stone circle, were not uncommon at one time. Robert Graves, in his famous book 'The White Goddess', commented on one such setting in Wales at Moelfre Hall, which was finally destroyed by the clergy in the seventeenth century. The stones were known as 'The Three Women' - supposedly petrified for winnowing corn on a Sunday! One of the stones was white, one red and one blue - a classic triple goddess setting. The fact that the clergy felt the need to destroy it seems to indicate the possibility at least that some vestiges of goddess worship lasted until that late date.

However, there is at least one triple goddess setting still surviving in all its glory and that is at Cnoc Fillibhear Bheag in the Hebrides, near Callanish in Lewis. Here there are three stones in ascending order of height from the whitish-coloured maiden, to the slightly taller red mother and the tallest darker-bluish old woman or hag. Facing them within the circle is the six foot tall, phallus-shaped male consort with whitish quartz at the top! That this setting in praise of the Great Mother Goddess has survived is undoubtedly a comment on its out-of-the-way location (see photograph on the following page).

It must be said that some of the most spectacular sacred sites in the landscape have resulted from the placement of stone circles close to hills that had been sacred for perhaps thousands of years. There are a number of spectacular examples around Britain and Ireland, but it is proposed to look at three in slightly more detail to discuss the particular atmosphere that seems to generate the sense of sacredness.

Cnoc Fillibhear Bheag, Lewis

Swinside (Cumbria).

This is certainly one of the most beautiful and atmospheric of the British stone circles. Its comparative remoteness has meant that it has been remarkably well preserved, with only a few stones removed. It rests in a hollow surrounded by beautiful hills, at the foot of the sacred 'breast - shaped' hill (see John Glover's beautiful photograph on the following page).

The circle is unusual in that it is placed on a thick bed of pebbles carried to the site, presumably to level it and to provide a foundation for the stones, of which fifty-five remain. The stones of the circle must have been fairly contiguous at one time, like a wall, with an entrance to the S.E. and a little 'porch way' of four stones. There is a tall 'male' stone set in the north and a squat 'female' one in the south.

Swinside means 'hillside of the pigs' and the alternative name for the circle is Sunkenkirk - a reference to the legend that the circle is the remains of the foundations of a church that the Devil pulled down each night as the builders tried to erect it during the day. Another attempt by the Church to tarnish the image of an ancient site!

Swinside and Sacred Hill at Dawn

A Spring Day at Swinside

The place has a wonderful atmosphere and was regularly used for 'pagan' rituals and festivities in the latter part of the twentieth century. The dowsed energy of the circle remains strong perhaps because of the isolated nature of the site and the large number of stones remaining. There are a number of concentric circles of energy as one moves towards the centre of the circle. A brief period of contemplation sitting on one of the perimeter stones evoked a spinning sensation as if the whole circle was about to 'take off'.

Castlerigg (Cumbria)

This is another of the great Cumbrian circles from the earliest period of stone circle construction in the Neolithic period, up to 5,200 years ago. Here again the setting is glorious with the surrounding mountains of the Lake District, including the Skiddaw range just to the north. The mountains were clearly sacred to our ancient forebears and this circle was built to celebrate this fact - in the mountains the people felt nearer to their god in a very real sense. The circle was obviously a religious, ritual centre, but it was also rather more, being involved in commerce and trade, particularly for the locally produced stone axes. If one thinks of a temple with a surrounding street market in a magnificent setting then that is probably fairly near the truth.

There are thirty-five stones remaining of the original forty-two and they are all made from the local Skiddaw slate. There is a distinct entrance in the north of two tall stones facing Skiddaw and there seems to be another entrance in the south-east overlooking the valley in which Thirlmere lake is situated. An unusual feature within this circle is an enclosure, abutting on the perimeter, in the east south-east.

The circle was alternatively known, although rarely nowadays, as the Carles, which is an ancient word meaning 'wise elders' - probably symbolic of how the stones were viewed all those thousands of years ago.

The atmosphere of the circle is truly wonderful, surrounded as it is by brooding mountains and it has many moods depending on the interplay of dense cloud, heavy rain, snow and bright sunshine. The following photographs illustrate the variations. More often than not, there are numerous sightseers at the circle and, perhaps because of the many visitors over the years, the dowsed energies at the site are nowhere near as strong as they are at Swinside. However there are enough to indicate that this was once a powerful focus of earth energies.

Castlerigg Stone Circle Circle, View from S.E. Entrance

Castlerigg Stone Circle -North Entrance Towards Clough Head

The Hurlers and the Cheesewring, Cornwall.

The Hurlers stone circles on Bodmin Moor are overlooked by the Cheesewring, a hill sacred to the Mesolithic and early Neolithic people (see previous chapter). This is one of the granite tors for which Bodmin Moor and Dartmoor are famous. The Cheesewring is a fantastically shaped hill which many people have described as apparently manmade. However it is granite weathered into wonderful shapes, perhaps modified by the ancients by the simple expedient of knocking down some carefully selected rocks. They also built a wall to enclose their sacred hill. Small wonder then that, at a later date, they built a great religious complex in its shadow.

The Hurlers themselves comprise three separate circles in a line, in varying stages of repair, or disrepair, as one of them only has nine stones remaining of an initial twenty-six. The largest circle is some forty-two metres across. The northern circle was originally paved in granite, an indication of religious usage. The alignment of the three circles is roughly from north-east to south-west. The centre circle is slightly egg-shaped and there are two standing stones, known as the Pipers, over one hundred metres to the W.S.W. of this circle.

The Church did its usual effective job of trying to deny the sanctity of the stones. The Hurlers circles are reputed to be either people petrified for dancing on the Sabbath, or for playing the game of hurling on the Sabbath. The Pipers were two men petrified for providing the musical accompaniment!

This whole complex up on Bodmin Moor is wonderfully atmospheric and includes barrows (including the Rillaton Barrow, source of a fabulous golden beaker), the circles, a stone row and enclosures. The weather must indeed have been warmer in the Neolithic period and into Bronze Age times.

The Rillaton Beaker

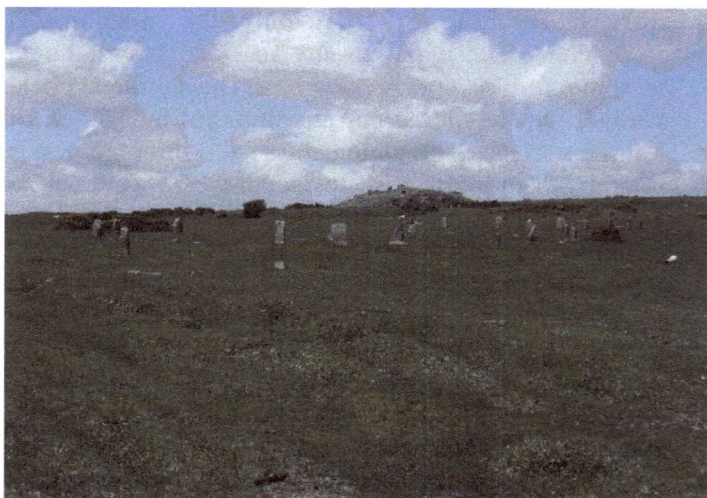

The Hurlers with the Cheesewring in the Background.

Castleden (1990) summed up neatly the close links between man and his environment and his clear view of the relationship with the heavens :-

"….. the circle is not only a moongate joining heaven and earth but also the hub about which the wheel of neolithic society slowly revolved. The ancestry of the stone circle, rooted in the earthen, broken circles of the early neolithic, was an ancient one and its development was long and complicated. Many grave mistakes have been made in attributing simple, single purposes to these great, subtle and many-sided projects.

They incorporate a bewildering matrix of symbols, beliefs and aspirations in their design, showing that they were used in a wide variety of ceremonial ways to express a holistic view of the universe, a view that saw no real division between man and nature, nor between earth and the heavens."

It will have been observed that the sites discussed to date tend to be located on the high moor lands or on the 'downland' of the chalk regions. Man had made a conscious decision to build his settlements rather than in the dense, wooded lowland valleys. This was not because he was frightened of the wild animals in the woods, as we were taught in our youth, but rather that, in the warmer, wetter climate of those times, the crops grew well on the hills and the domesticated animals could be protected from the wild animals more easily. There is also the important point that man had a sense of closeness with the heavens and spirit on the hills - to use a Christian expression 'nearer my God to thee' and it was here that earth and heaven had their closest conjunction. Hence, as already mentioned, the standing stones and circles pointed skywards to the 'above'. This can be likened to the towers and steeples in cathedrals and churches pointing to the sky, conducting the 'light' to the congregation. Burial mounds, dolmens, barrows etc. were often built in prominent locations, again placing the dead people, the ancestors, closer to Heaven at the start of the journey towards rebirth.

We have so far examined sacred sites almost as if they sprang into being almost fully developed but logically there must have been some common point of origin.

The Development and Location of Sacred Sites.

It is clear from the outset that sacred sites are a universal phenomenon. Pyramids, stone circles and standing stones (monoliths) are found world wide - North , Central and South America, Britain and Europe, Egypt and the Middle East, and throughout Asia and Polynesia. They were all clearly erected by people who knew about sacred geometry, angles of slope etc. and they were all built with one sole purpose in mind - the glorification of the Great Spirit in one form or another. It is also obvious that the local races did not have the technology, at least initially, to carry out such work, and that this was probably carried out by a 'master' race who settled all over the world. Some people have postulated that these people fled from the destruction of their homeland in the Atlantic Ocean (the Atlanteans) and others from a similar centre in the Pacific Ocean (the Lemurians). Wherever they came from, and many interested scholars favour the Atlantic Ocean as being the resting place of Atlantis, if they did spread out from two centres then they must have been from one group originally since the available knowledge and designs are so similar. It is apparent that the basic blueprint for e.g. pyramids was similar in all cases but with local variations perhaps applied by the indigenous peoples or as a result of variations in available building material. One could perhaps cite the pyramids of Egypt built with massive blocks of limestone and those of Tenerife built of the local lava. Michell (1983) wrote :-

"A great scientific instrument lies sprawled over the entire surface of the globe. At some period, thousands of years ago, almost every corner of the world was visited by people with a particular task to accomplish.

With the help of some remarkable power, by which they could cut and raise enormous blocks of stone, these men created vast astronomical instruments, circles of erect pillars, pyramids, underground tunnels, cyclopean stone platforms, all linked together by a network of tracks and alignments, whose course from horizon to horizon was marked by stones,mounds and earthworks." (p.83)

However, all these great monuments, mostly constructed within a comparatively short period of time in prehistoric times were not built where they were at the whim of the builders or 'architects'. As explained previously, the sites were in a special sense 'sacred' and our distant ancestors could sense a form of earth energy in such locations that led them to position many of their great centres where they did. We have constantly made the mistake of underestimating and under valuing our forebears, they had a brain capacity similar to our own and possessed abilities - spiritual, psychic and mental - that the vast majority of modern people can only dream about. The whole issue of earth energies and the associated topic of ley lines will be discussed in some detail in Chapter 5.

It seems clear from the preceding pages that our ancient, 'pagan' ancestors had a clear view of their environment and the relationship between the earth ('below') and the sky, or heavens ('above'). They took great care to propitiate the gods or spirit that ruled over the domain in which they lived. They realised too that the two realms were indivisibly linked and that their live on earth depended upon the bounty of the heavens - the warmth, the light and the rainfall. They saw that the sun, moon and stars were important energy sources and pointers to the course of the year - the alignment of their circles and stones in the landscape reflected this.

Chapter Four
Temples of Sun, Moon and Stars

Controversy has raged for more than two hundred and fifty years concerning the potential astronomical purpose of the stone circles and monoliths, with archaeologists and archaeo - astronomers tending to line up on opposite sides of the divide.

Stukeley, in 1740, wrote that Stonehenge was aligned to the north-east "whereabouts the sun rises, when the days are longest." In the present day, Hawkins, in his 'Stonehenge Decoded' (1966), set out to prove the numerous alignments at Stonehenge using a computer to tabulate all his measurements. Despite the volume of evidence he produced, his work has still been challenged on the twofold basis that, firstly, he set out to prove the alignments and hence all his evidence was positive and, secondly, that the short range of many of the sight lines meant that there was a margin of error in most of his measurements.

Even Bord and Bord (1986), great believers in the spiritual power of the ancient monuments, seem somewhat cynical as to the astronomical significance of the stones:-

"Whether all this was done in order to construct an observatory capable of many complex astronomical observations, as some of today's computer-addicted scientists would like to think, is still open to conjecture." (page 14 - 'Earth Rites', 1982).

However the work of Professor Thom, with his training as an engineer, on the shape of stone circles and his careful measurement of the alignment to sun, moon and stars seems to prove that there can be no doubt at all that one of the purposes of the circles was to indicate certain alignments at certain times of the year, such as the equinoxes and the solstices. The main controversy that remains lies in the purpose of all these astronomical measurements.

Hawkins (1966 put a threefold motivation forward for the alignments :-

"The Stonehenge sun/moon alignments were created and elaborated for two, possibly three, reasons: they made a calendar, particularly useful to tell the time for planting crops, they helped to create and maintain priestly power, by enabling the priest to call out the multitude to see the spectacular risings and settings of the sun and moon, most especially the midsummer sunrise over the heelstone and midwinter sunset through the great trilithon, and possibly they served as an intellectual game."

It is difficult to accept that local people, working hard to grow their crops and rear their animals, would have been prepares to devote hundreds of thousands of man hours to the construction of these monuments in the interests of an intellectual game devised by the shaman.

Likewise, it is hard to accept that the

monuments were constructed simply to act as a calendar to tell people when to plant their crops. Neolithic man was far more in touch with nature than his modern counterpart - he would have noted the days becoming longer and sensed the right conditions for planting the crops. True a calendar would have provided supporting evidence but this cannot have been the main purpose of the alignments.

There is some possibility that there was an element of showmanship on the part of the priests being able to foretell the shortest day or the most northerly position of moonrise and to 'put on a show' for the people.

However, there can be little doubt that the main purpose of the alignments in a stone circle was concerned with the serious business of ritual and worship of the sun god and moon goddess - it is worth remembering that the sun was regarded as masculine and the moon as feminine. For thousands of years of goddess worship the moon was seen as pre-eminent, however the move to the growing of crops and the resulting greater significance of the male labour force in the tilling of the land, planting and harvesting brought to the fore the importance of the sun. The moon goddess took on a slightly lesser role as the goddess of the harvest. Hence, at many sites, the alignments to both the sun and the moon became vitally important, so that the ritual could be directed at the God/Goddess at the appropriate time. It is possible that alignments to the stars were also considered to be important, sometimes as an early warning of a significant sun or moon alignment, sometimes in their own right as an object of worship, such as Venus.

Establishing and setting out the alignments must have been a technical and lengthy task for the shaman and his labour force. The solstitial and equinoctial sunrise and sunsets must have been difficult enough, but the measurements for the Moon and Venus must have been spread over several years, even generations, and demonstrates a degree of planning that modern generations might not have expected. Concerning the establishing of the alignments, Michell (1983) points out:-

"In many cases, stones are set outside the circles, forming alignments which point to a natural hill or mountain peak, to a stone or mound placed on the horizon or to a notch cut through a high ridge visible on the skyline. Only from the site of the stone circle itself have these works any significance, for they marked the spots where the sun appeared or vanished at the equinox or at the solstices or where the moon reaches an extreme position in one of its complicated cycles." (page 46).

An important point is being made here - the need for outlying markers to view the alignments. If a person standing in the middle of the circle has a distant marker, then there is less room for error, a more accurate reading than if the marker is near to the circle or indeed part of the ring itself. Many of the sacred sites discussed in this book have clear outlying markers of the type discussed above, noteworthy examples would include Kilmartin Glen (the famous Nether Largie five stone setting), Castlerigg and Bryn Celli-ddu.

In the Orkneys, quite a complex arrangement of alignments can be found around Maes Howe, the Stones of Stenness and the Ring of Brodgar, and the monoliths known as the Watchstone and the Barnstone. The setting sun at the midwinter solstice shines down the entrance passage of Maes Howe and, viewed from the latter, the winter sun sets over the Barnstone. These two events are pictured on the following page.

As to the complex of alignments at this location, Devereux comments :-

"These alignments, plus others involving the nearby Stones of Stenness circle, between them aligned to sunrise or sunset points variously, on both of the solstices, each of the equinoxes, plus the old Celtic cylindrical days of Beltane (May Day) and Samhain ……….." (page 138).

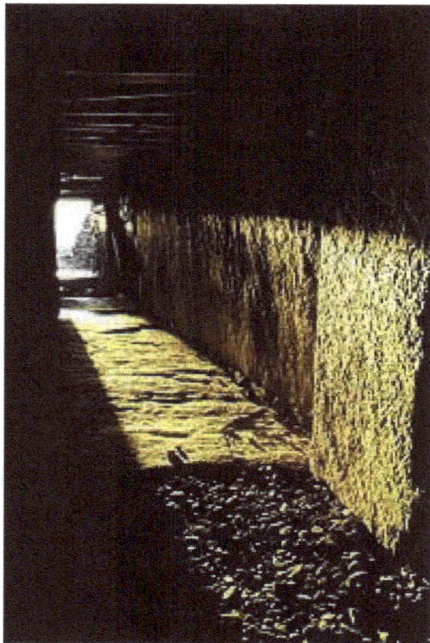

Midwinter Sunset at Maes Howe

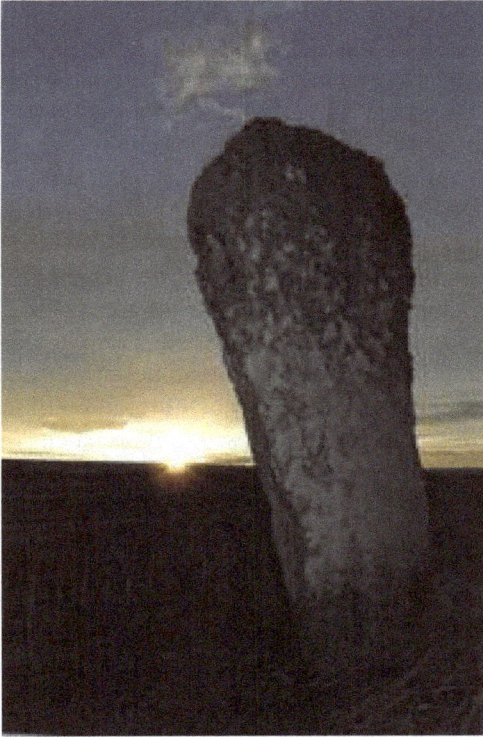

Midwinter Sunset over the Barnstone.
(pictures printed with the permission of Charles Tait.)

The fact that the stones predate the Celtic calendar would seem to indicate that festivals such as Beltane and Samhain predated the Celts, at least as far as the celebration of the actual day is concerned, if not in name. It is likely that some of the alignments at a few circles were used to predict solar and lunar eclipses. It is interesting that a huge complex of temples and dwellings is being excavated in the area. In the minds of our Neolithic ancestors, it is quite possible that an eclipse was considered to be an ominous sign - much like 'the end of the world is nigh'. It is probable that some form of priestly showmanship came into play here. If the priest knew the day of an eclipse, then he could set up a suitable ritual ceremony whereby the eclipse would be ended, ensuring the safety of the group until the next event. In the same way, there would be great comfort in the knowledge that, following the winter solstice, the daylight period would gradually start to become longer again.

All of these points must be seen against the background of the fact that the stone circles and many of the other monuments of the Neolithic were places of worship - temples - and as such were the focus of the lives of the local inhabitants. As indicated elsewhere in this book, these lives, on the spiritual side at least, were dedicated to the worship of the Goddess and, latterly, the God, and also to the worship of the ancestors and the cycle of death and rebirth. The alignment to the sunrise and sunset at the winter solstice fits into the idea of rebirth as a portent of the arrival of spring.

Whilst the ancients did not have a calendar in the modern meaning of the word, they did have a method for calculating the days of their great religious festivals. These festivals were not on dates such as Christmas Day and certainly not the 'moveably feast' of Easter, as in the Christian calendar, although it is true that these Christian dates were fixed to roughly coincide with the earlier 'Pagan' festivals. These celebrations were all about the longest and shortest days of the year, or on nights when the moonrise was at its its limits in its 18.6 year cycle. They were about the warmth of the sun and the rain making their crops grow and those crops being ready for harvesting in due time. They were also all about the spirits of the dead, the ancestors, and facilitating their move into the spirit world, or calling them back to make use of their wisdom in guiding the future life of the group.

Castleden (1998) believes that the solstices represented times of crisis to our ancestors - times when changes would take place in the course of the year. Hence the solstices were times when people would gather at the circles to be initiated into this new period of their lives.

"The magic circles thus take on another function as liminal refuges for whole communities during solstitial crises. In this respect, it is useful to apply to the circles the idea of intense statelessness that was seen in the individual rites of passage. The boundary, whatever it is, is a place that is not a place, in a time that is not a time

.... These were moments when the great occult wisdom of the community was realised and the deep knowledge of the basic structure of their culture came home to people." (page 241).

It does seem that the alignments in most cases were related to the sun and the moon and were meant to be generally predictive rather than specific. As Castleden says, of stone circles, the 'orientation was celebratory and magical rather than scientific, unless there is some reason for believing that accuracy was sought at a particular circle.' (pages 153-154).

It is proposed to look briefly at the alignments detected at a number of the sites mentioned elsewhere in this book and then to look in greater detail at those two great sites, Stonehenge and Callanish.

Major Alignments
1/ Castlerigg (Cumbria).

Here a tall slender pillar, set sideways on within the circle, lies in the S.E. of the circle. This is aligned to sunrise in February at the festival of Imbolc, the sun rises between the high fells of Matterdale Common, three miles away. The following photograph by John Glover also shows the shadow cast by the tallest stone in the circle at midsummer sunset.

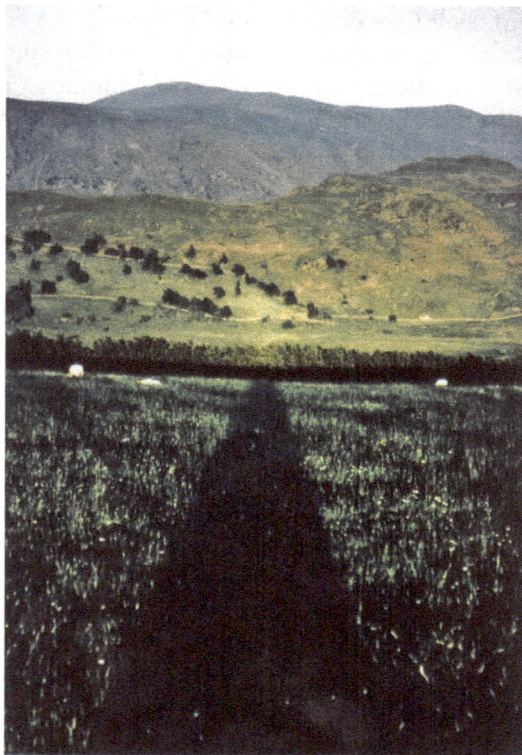

Castlerigg Sunset Shadow by John Glover

2/ Long Meg and Her Daughters (Cumbria).
An alignment through Long Meg from the centre of the circle indicates the midwinter sunset, the following photograph taken by John Glover shows the shadow of Long Meg stretched across the circle.

The Shadow of Long Meg by John Glover

3/ Swinside (Cumbria).
Here the alignment from the circle across the two southernmost stones of the entrance is at an angle of 134.5 degrees, which indicates midwinter sunrise.
Burl in 'Circles of Stone' (Milligan and Burl, 1999) paints a graphic picture of the scene :-
"...... an open space, where a hundred or more people assembled at the blackest, emptiest part of the year. Only imagination can tell us what ceremonies they performed, what their fears were. No more than

71

the stones survive." (page 67).

4/ Arbor Low (Derbyshire).
This is a major complex for this part of England. It is probable that the central cove was built first. There seems to be a focus on death and fertility and the cove points towards the major northern sunrise to the north-east. The death aspect is supported by the presence of eight chambered tombs within the local area.

5/ Rollright (Oxfordshire).
A wonderful stone circle in central England. It has a damaged, portalled entrance in the south-east pointing to the major southern moonrise.

6/ Stonehenge (Wiltshire).
It would appear from the work done by the archaeo-astronomers, such as Professors Thom and Hawkins, with their computers and complex measurements, that the use of the circle for astronomical measurements dates from about 1800 B.C.E. Alignments have been claimed for stars such as Capella and the Pleiades, but two questions must be considered. Firstly, how accurate can such alignments be? Secondly, why would the ancients want to observe such systems? The answer to the first question would seem to be that we would need to know the exact date of such a potential alignment to check its accuracy, given the movement of the star systems around the sky over the centuries. No practical answer can be given to the second question beyond the idea that the shamans perceived some form of link between the particular star and themselves.

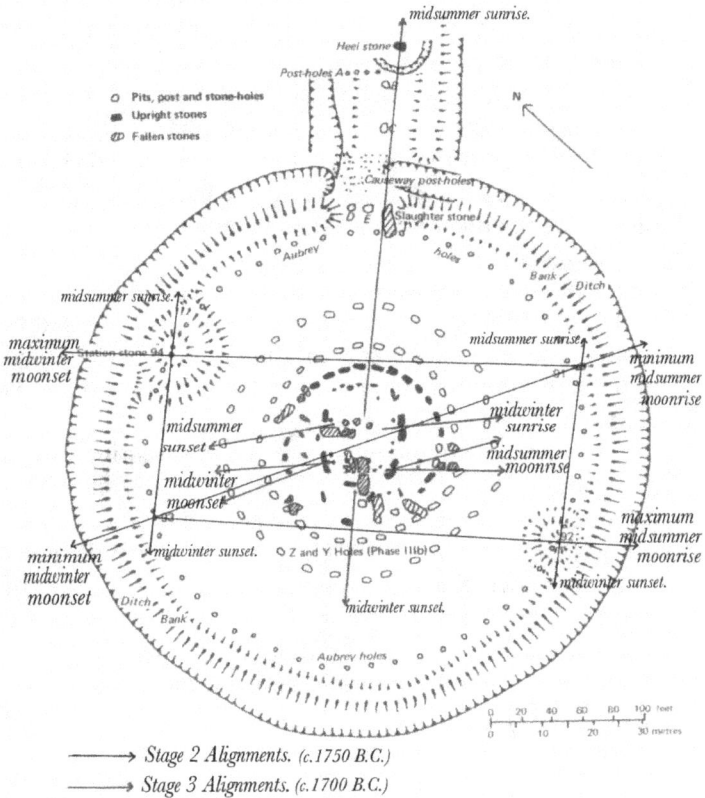

midsummer sunrise.

Heel stone

Post-holes A

N

O Pits, post and stone-holes
Upright stones
Fallen stones

Causeway post-holes

Slaughter stone

Aubrey

holes

Bank Ditch

midsummer sunrise.

maximum
midwinter   Station stone 94
moonset

midsummer sunrise

minimum
midsummer
moonrise

midsummer
sunset

midwinter
sunrise

midsummer
moonrise

midwinter
moonset

maximum
midsummer
moonrise

minimum
midwinter
moonset

midwinter sunset.   Z and Y Holes (Phase IIIb)

midwinter sunset.

Ditch

Bank

midwinter sunset.

Aubrey holes

0   20   40   60   80   100 feet

0   10   20   30 metres

$\longrightarrow$ *Stage 2 Alignments. (c.1750 B.C.)*
$\longrightarrow$ *Stage 3 Alignments. (c.1700 B.C.)*

Based on Hadingham (1976), in turn taken from Hawkins (Fontans Books, 1970) -'Stonehenge Decoded'.

Accordingly, it has been decided to focus upon the
more obvious alignments to the sun and moon, as
depicted on the above map, as these were clearly the
chief objects of the worship of the ancients.
Alignments to prominent stars such as Venus,
particularly at Newgrange, and its eight year cycle,
are sufficiently rare not to have been included.
The Stonehenge map (above), based on Hadingham

(1976) and Hawkins (1970) shows the alignments to the sun and moon at Stonehenge. It demonstrates how the alignments changed between the second phase of the construction of the circle in c. 1750 B.C.E. and the third phase in c. 1700 B.C.E. The second phase alignments were based on a rectangle of four stones based on the circle of so-called Aubrey Holes, which were placed just inside the line of the original henge.

Sitings between these stones, as indicated on the map, point to midsummer sunrise and sunset and midwinter sunrise and sunset. They can also be used to predict the maximum and minimum midsummer and midwinter moonrise and moonset, i.e. when the moon is at the end of its 18.6 year cycle.

The stage 3 alignments were based on sitings from the stones of the circle itself - most especially the siting through the great trilithon towards the midsummer sunrise over the heel, or hele, stone - although many people believe that there would have been a pair of stones with the sun rising between them. On the opposite alignment, the midwinter sunset could be observed on the all-important shortest day of the year. Other important phases of the sun and moon could be predicted by other alignments across the stones.

7/ Callanish.

The main circle at Callanish has been dated as being over four thousand years old. It started with a single main megalith, about 4,500 years ago and then, about three hundred years later, the surrounding circle of stones was added. Finally came the avenue and the stone rows, giving the appearance of a deformed celtic cross (see accompanying map in a couple of pages). At a later time, in common with many other sacred sites (such as at

Kilmartin Glen on Scotland's west coast), a miniature chambered cairn was placed within the circle, in this case between the central stone and the eastern edge of the circle. About three thousand years ago, the site was abandoned, probably as the climate became cooler and wetter. Peat deposits built up, reaching about two metres by the early nineteenth century, rendering the majority of the stones invisible. It must be remembered that Callanish 1, as it has been termed, is just one site within a great complex of Neolthic sites within a very small area. Eleven other sites have been given a Callanish designation by G. and M. Ponting (1977), thus going up to Callanish XII. Numerous alignments between these sites have been identified by Professor Thom, mainly of important solar and lunar phases.

It is clear that the climate in the late Neolithic/early Bronze ages must have been drier and warmer than that experienced nowadays. The latest information from Margaret Curtis is that the Callanish situation is even more complex than first pictured. The northern corridor of Callanish I has been extended further north and has been aligned with another circle up on the hill. Much work clearly needs to be done. Folk tales tell of people arriving by boat, led by a priest-king clad in a plumed cloak and accompanied by other priests. There were 'black men' with them who erected the stones.Most of the people then sailed away, leaving behind the priest-king and a number of others. This folk tale sounds remarkably like the 'legends' of the survivors of the fall of Atlantis.

The alignments at the main Callanish site, being mainly short, provide a general view of e.g. the midwinter sunset, but may not be called, by any means, astronomically accurate. As G. and M. Ponting comment in their booklet 'The Standing Stones of Callanish (1977) :-

"With two stones only a few yards apart, a fairly wide section of the horizon is indicated. If the two markers are, instead, several miles apart, the accuracy is greatly improved. This may be the reason why there are so many sites in the Callanish area - the significant alignments may be from one site to another." (page 25).

The importance of the alignments at Callanish is that they provided very significant lunar observations. Latitude plays an important role in the nature of the observations that can be made. At Stonehenge, for instance, the latitude is really more suited to solar alignments, but at Callanish, much further north, lunar observations are more significant. "For a few days, in each 18.61 years, the moon rises so close to due south that its path across the sky (from rise at W to set at X in the following diagram) is less than two degrees above the horizon. In other words the full moon just skims above the horizon." (ibid, page 20.).

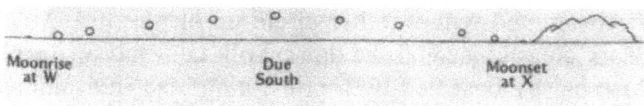

Callanish 1
(Printed with the permission of Margaret Curtis)

Professor Thom believed that lunar alignments were often achieved by using distant mountains and notches as sight lines, lined up with the stones. In this way, he believed that the slight wobble (nine degrees) in the moon's orbit was measured by the ancients.

76

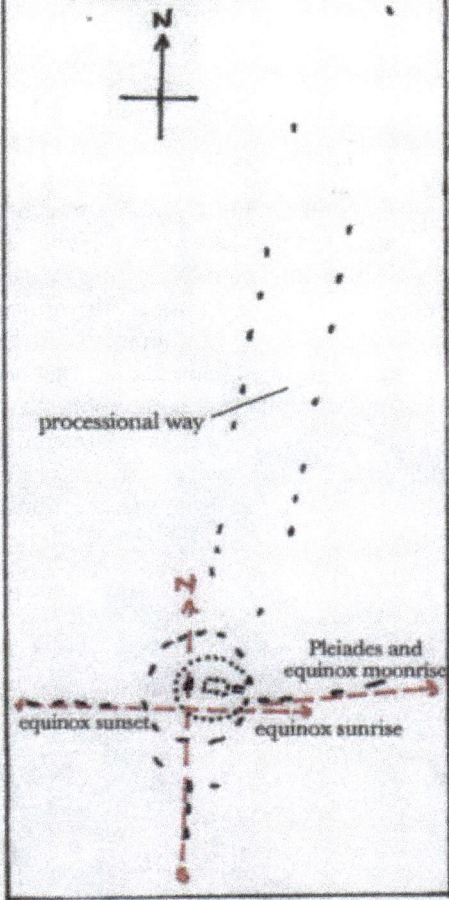

Alignments at Callanish 1.

N

processional way

N

Pleiades and equinox moonrise

equinox sunset

equinox sunrise

S

As to the alignment of the rows, they appear to be general rather than precise. The southern row is laid out in a clear north - south alignment.

The western row, viewed from the end looking back eastwards through the circle is aligned to the sunrise at the equinoxes and, looking westwards is aligned to the sunset at the equinoxes. The eastern row has its flat faced slabs lined up pointing to the Pleiades (at about 1750 B.C.E. according to Somerville) and to the moonrise at the equinoxes (Hawkins). Professor Thom sees the alignment as being capable of being used for both purposes. It is extremely likely that these alignments were used with other monuments in the complex to achieve more accurate readings on the sun and moon. Once again, it is astounding to contemplate the ingenuity of the priests and the hard work of the people in constructing these mighty sites over four thousand years ago.

Callanish 1
Printed with the permission of Margaret Curtis

It is quite clear that, certainly in the early Bronze Age, the circles and megaliths, often in conjunction with the surrounding landscape, were used to foretell the location of the sun and moon in the sky at particular times of the year. This probably also applied to certain star systems, such as Venus and the Pleiades, at particular locations such as Newgrange (in Ireland), Stonehenge and Callanish. Some of these alignments could be measured precisely where long site lines were used, and others were for more general usage.

As Ponting and Ponting (1977) state :-
"All of this presumes a much greater intellect for prehistoric man than previously supposed. But his brain size was equal to ours - there is no real reason to regard him as less capable of abstract mathematical thought than we are." (page 18).

However we must remember that sites were sacred long before the alignments were devised. Stone circles and chambered cairns were used by the ancestors to worship the Goddess - they were temples to the natural order of things, as described in the two previous chapters. They were also to connect mankind with the realm of spirit - mostly those of the ancestors - in other words living with the 'dead'.

As Castleden (1998) states in clearly spiritual terms :- "The ring of votive pits at Stonehenge implies a dedication to earth, while the stones of the Ring of Brodgar, soaring heavenward, imply a dedication to sky. At many sites, one has a sense that the ring of stones fastens the two worlds together and makes a moongate through which we can step from world to world." (page 152).

79

The dedication to the sun and the moon must be seen as part of the evolution of the prehistoric spirituality – a continuation of what had gone before. Mankind still worshipped the ancestors but the worship of the Goddess had been replaced by reverence for the Sun God (heaven) and the Moon Goddess (earth) as the providers of the conditions for the growth of their food. The temples had simply extended their functions to provide a focus for that worship at particular times of the year. It is just a tragedy that, as society became increasingly male dominated, the worship of the moon goddess became subsidiary to that of the sun god, eventually becoming virtually totally eclipsed.

Chapter Five
The Natural Grid System

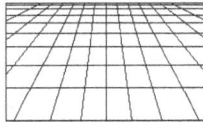

In 1921, Alfred Watkins, a Hampshire flour miller, riding around the county on horseback, paused on a hilltop and experienced one of those 'intuitive' flashes of insight that we all receive from time to time. He realised that many of the prominent man - made features of the landscape were laid out in straight lines across the countryside. He distinguished many features that could be included on these 'leys' as he termed them (strictly speaking, a 'ley' is a cleared glade or a patch of open ground.).

Michell (1983, page 23) described the moment of Watkins's enlightenment in lyrical terms :-

"Watkins saw straight through the surface of the landscape to a layer deposited in some remote prehistoric age. The barrier of time melted and spread across the country, he saw a web of lines linking the holy places and sites of antiquity.

Mounds, old stones, crosses and old crossroads, churches placed on pre - Christian sites, legendary trees, moats and holy wells stood in exact alignments that ran over beacon hills to cairns and mountain peaks. In one moment of transcendental perception Watkins entered a magic world of prehistoric Britain, a world whose very existence had been forgotten."

It should be recognised that straight lines in the landscape have been a feature of life of the ancient peoples all over the world, notably including Peru (the Nazca lines), Bolivia, North America, Europe and Australia. In China, the geomantic method of 'feng shui' evolved with the terrestrial energies being known as the 'dragon currrent'. In China, the aim was to find the best location for a site rather than laying them out in straight lines, for it was believed that malign influences travel along such lines and therefore they are to be avoided at all costs.

Watkins's perception was that the straight lines were originally prehistoric pathways with the other features then placed along them, and he eventually published his findings in a book entitled 'The Old Straight Track'. His work was enthusiastically received and many groups were set up in the 1920s and 1930s to seek out and discuss the new alignments of sites that had been discovered. The Second World War saw a great decline in research but interest was rekindled in the 1950s and 1960s and on to the present day with many of the great names in 'earth mysteries', such as Paul Devereux and John Michell being involved. It is fair to say that the concept of leys has been altered and considerably expanded in the eighty years since Watkins originally proposed the idea.

There is now general agreement among 'ley hunters' that Watkins was incorrect in his belief that leys marked the lines of ancient track ways, although it is undoubtedly true that many prehistoric tracks did follow the leys. A ley is only considered established when it links at least four sites in a straight line on the large scale Ordnance Survey map of the area - in this case it is clear that lengths of old track way, often in the shape of footpaths, lanes and even roads do indeed follow straight along the line of the ley.

There are two chief theories concerning the placement of leys on the landscape. Watkins originally considered that leys were laid out by 'line of sight' from one point to another in order to maintain the straightness of the lines - in other words prehistoric man wanted to get from A to B in a straight line and used a sort of ranging pole method to plot the line. This he might then have marked by cairns, monoliths, earth mounds etc. - it is worth remembering that not every 'tumulus' that has been excavated has contained a burial and perhaps could be markers. There is also a belief, common amongst modern researchers, that, whilst many leys may have been laid out using the above method, many were in fact laid out following the pattern of energy currents within the earth. These energy currents followed lines of stress in the earth's crust, i.e. fault lines, and therefore tended to be straight. By this method, it should be understood that stone circles and monoliths were not simply placed as markers but were also there to actually *boost the energy.* Ancient man, more in touch with nature and the earth energies than his modern equivalent, was able to 'read' the energy and lay out his sacred sites accordingly. A stone circle then has another aspect beyond the religion, the ritual and the astronomy, it could also be likened to a booster generating station on the national electricity grid system. The term 'geomancy' has come to be used when referring to the sacred layout of the landscape.

There was a long held belief among archaeologists that our 'pagan' ancestors were primitive savages incapable of rational thought as we think of it today. However increasingly evidence is accruing that they lived a better, more harmonious life than had been believed possible. They dressed better than had been supposed and had a better diet. In addition to this, perhaps because of their less frenetic existence, they were far more closely in touch with the natural world and likewise in tune with the spirit world and particularly with the spirits of their ancestors. The ancient sacred sites provided foci for these links with spirits. The stone circles, monoliths, long barrows, fogous and other similar locations were seen as places where the physical world and the spirit world could draw closer through the mediumship of the priest/shamans - in other words these were places where the veils between the worlds was at its thinnest. A stone circle with its powerful energies (remember the spinning sensation experienced at Swinside) was a gateway to the spirit realms where the shamans could bring the spirits closer to the people - Stonehenge was the greatest gate in this respect. A line of such sites would focus the energies more strongly and, as we shall see in Chapter 7, further increased the flow of energy to the circles.

Sullivan (1999, p.76) states :-

In the ancient past, the tribal priest or shaman would have been one such psychically gifted individual, and it was his role to commune with the spirits of the ancestors in order to gain insight and guidance. What begins to emerge here is how the concept of 'spirit' has been absorbed into the concept of 'energy' over the years. Four thousand years ago people would have visited the stones and the sacred places in the hope that their ancestors or spirits would help and guide them ......" Nowadays, people such as the shamans who made the spirit world available to the people are called mediums and it is a shameful thing that, in the intervening centuries, such people have been persecuted by the Church and sentenced to death by burning at the stake or drowned on the ducking stool, or pursued by the officers of the civil law, as was the case with Helen Duncan as recently as the 1940s.

In modern terms, leys may be likened to a laser beam linking up a number of sites in the landscape, as stated previously, four or more are considered necessary to minimise the possibility of random alignments, in a dead straight line with no room for deviation. Such leys are not usually more than a few miles in length. A famous example of a typical ley, as evidenced by Devereux and Thompson (1979) and Sullivan (1999), is the Silbury Hill ley in Wiltshire. This runs for thirteen miles through Avebury and Silbury Hill, linking Bincknoll Castle in the north and Maiden Henge in the south with six points on the ley between these two.

However, as already indicated, many leys have been dowsed and found to be constructed along lines of earth energy, either where the energy is able to follow a fault line in the earth's crust or an underground water course. The latter may be the reason why some apparent leys are not quite straight. There is also the intriguing probability that prehistoric people were able to use stone circles and monoliths to send energy across country *above* the surface, by building up the energy in the stones and in some way directing it elsewhere. Tom Graves, a modern dowser, has carried out much work proving the existence of these 'overgrounds' as he calls them (see diagrams on the following page).

Janet and Colin Bord (1982, page 228) have this comment to make :-

"Standing stones have been found to carry 'charges' (the nature of this force or energy is still unknown, hence the difficulty in naming it) which are sometimes so powerful that the dowser is thrown back from a stone when he touches it. Also, pulses of energy have been measured travelling from stone to stone around a stone circle, or long distances across country as overgrounds from one site to another."

Tom Graves realised that the monoliths were used by the ancient people to control the flow of terrestrial energy. The following diagrams show two examples of how earth energies were directed out from monoliths and stone circles. The first diagram shows the dowsing lines around the Cuckoo Stone, a monolith near to Woodhenge in Wiltshire (the dowsing lines have been considerably simplified). The second diagram is based on work carried out on the so - called Dragon Project, led by Paul Devereux, at the Rollwright Stones in Oxfordshire.

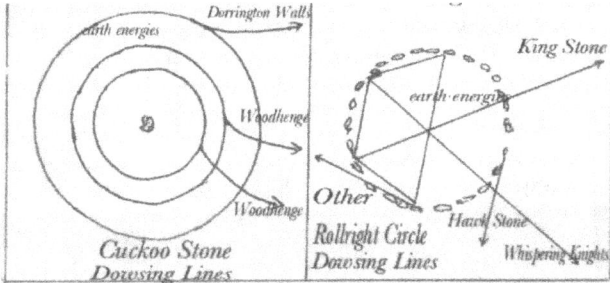

Cuckoo Stone Dowsing Lines | Other Rollright Circle Dowsing Lines

Adapted from Sullivan (1999)

It is interesting that Graves also noted that a similar effect, namely the build up of energies, came from maypoles, used in the same fashion as monoliths, but in this case the energy was built up by the frantic dancing of the local people around the maypole. This must represent an interesting throwback to the ancients dancing around the stone circle or monolith to add to their energy. Michell (1983) noted a similar effect derived from the traditional dancing that used to take place into historic times around old churches. The example he cites was at Rede Church in Somerset. We shall see in Chapter 6 how many churches were built inside stone circles - so this is probably another throwback to rituals that took place in prehistoric times.

In respect of these 'normal', comparatively short leys, one can picture a small tribal, or family, group, with their shaman laying out their sacred landscape, within their own territory, either using the line of sight method or following the energy along a ley and erecting stones or other sacred elements at significant points along the line.

Although this is not specifically a book about

leys, they do impinge on the study because of their association with major sacred sites. It is proposed therefore to illustrate some important leys that include sites mentioned elsewhere in this volume (see diagrams in Appendix B).

Michell (1983,page 53) has also compared the design of the early Gothic - style churches and cathedrals, introduced into western Europe by the Knights Templar, to walking along a typical wooded ley. We will make further mention of the Templars later in the chapter. The design of the buildings was such that it imitated the grandeur of the trees in the woodland with the light filtering through the branches. He pictured the traveller moving along the tracks through the trees, shaded but in dappled sunlight.

"It was this state of spiritual tranquillity that the architects of Gothic churches and cathedrals set out to recreate through their buildings. As late as the Middle Ages those who understood the magic science of invoking the spirits of revelation and ecstasy set up the naves, passages and cloisters of their great cathedrals to reproduce the harmonious proportions of a forest ride. The eye is drawn down the avenue between the pillars towards a veiled light far away at the east window.

Overhead the vaulted ribs of the roof, meeting at knots of carved foliage, spring out from the great stone trunks. Through the subtle, broken patterns of stained glass windows the light is diffused like that of a forest glade. Strange, twisted faces peer from among the leaves and flowers carved on the pillars and roof and above the windows. These spirits of trees and plant .... must once have been instantly recognised: the forest spirits, an inseparable part until recent centuries of the visible quality of every bush and tree."

This would appear to have been another way in which memories of the past were preserved under the noses of the established church. It accounts for the presence of 'green men' in so many churches across Britain - representing the spirit of nature, the dying and rising again God (Tammuz, Osiris, Herne the Hunter, Jack o'the Green, among the many names he has been given over the centuries) and the old religion.

It cannot be stressed too much how important the energy of the sacred sites must have been to our ancient ancestors and the fact that the leys were to convey the energy from place to place and to boost it in the process - exactly as our electricity grid system does nowadays. We have subsidiary generating sites feeding more electricity into the national system.

In any discussion of sacred sites and leys, it is worth remembering that many of the lines run through streams, ponds and lakes and must indeed pick up energies from the moving water. Lakes and crossing places in rivers were often considered to be sacred sites by the ancient peoples and, as such were regularly used as places where offerings of gifts to the Great Spirit (gods) could be made, gifts such as swords, shields and other valuable objects. This was probably the origin of the story of the Lady of the Lake in the Arthurian romances. In some cultures, sacrifices were made, both human and animal, at such places and lakes and streams were also used on occasion for the burial of war leaders, often in lead lined coffins.

It should be noted too that the trees and woodland may have been used to 'top up' the energy.

The Druids carried out many of their rituals in woodland clearings, because of the energies present in the very air and vegetation around them. As an example, the ley that runs through Rosslyn Chapel and on to Queens Ferry on the Firth of Forth, had Temple Wood in the shape of a Templar cross planted astride it. This was obviously designed to link into and maximise the energy flow.

There can be little dispute about the existence of deliberate leys across the countryside, varying in length from a few miles to more than twenty. The examples illustrated in Appendix B show beyond coincidence that our ancestors laid out these sites in straight lines. However we have not yet discussed the nature of the energy that is to be found along these lines.

The Earth's Energy
The Earth is a mass of energy - it is, as we know, a huge magnet with its own 'north' and 'south' poles with all the currents of power we have seen demonstrated in a bar magnet (as illustrated in the following diagram).

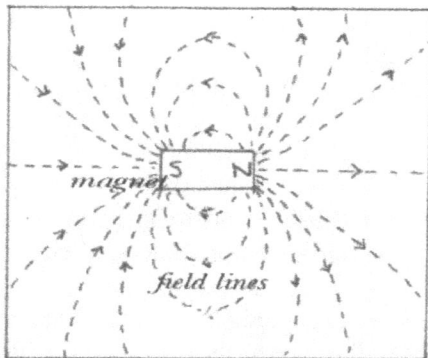

However the pattern of energies associated with the Earth is not smooth as we see in the bar magnet. The magnetic energy of Earth is affected by a number of factors such as the proximity of other heavenly bodies, including the Sun and moon as well as the planets. It is also affected by the nature of the landscape and the geology, with low, flat land having a smooth, uninterrupted current, but on a rugged landscape it becomes more dynamic, more disturbed. In places where there are geological faults, the energies become particularly agitated and it is at locations such as these that the energies break through on the surface. Whilst modern scientists know something about the influence on the magnetic energies of the Earth, sunspot activity and their effect on meteorological conditions, they do not as yet understand its nature and effect. Yet, as Michell (1983) puts it :-

"....... the evidence from the remote past points to the conclusion that earth's natural magnetism was not only known to man some thousands of years ago but provided them with a source of energy and inspiration to which their whole civilisation was tuned." (p.84).

It is quite clear that the old picture of prehistoric men being savages forced to live on hilltops because of their fear of the wild animals in the wooded valleys is a total misconception. Surely it is the case that our Neolithic forebears lived on the hills because the energies were more in evidence here and also the sites were more intervisible, making communication across distance more viable. We have constantly made the mistake of underestimating and undervaluing our distant ancestors - they had a brain capacity similar to ours and possessed abilities, spiritual, psychic and mental, that the vast majority of modern people can only dream about.

Guy Underwood did considerable work dowsing for the hidden energies and currents in the earth. The results of this scientific exploration he presented in his book 'Patterns of the Past' in 1969. He stated that most of the natural features of prehistoric geography were sited at prominent points of this subterranean energy. For instance, stone circles were created over what he called 'blind springs' - strong sources of energy. Poynder, in his 1992 book, 'Pi in the Sky', clarifies the point about blind springs, referring to them as underground water junctions. He further makes the point that the energy forms a spiral from the blind spring up to the surface and that the depth of the blind spring determines the radius of the stone circle on the surface, as illustrated in the following diagram. The spiral of energy is important and Poynder asserts that the spiral sign was placed by ancient man next to water points all over the world and indeed it can be seen at a great many stone circles in Britain, e.g. Long Meg in Cumbria, Temple Wood in Argyll.

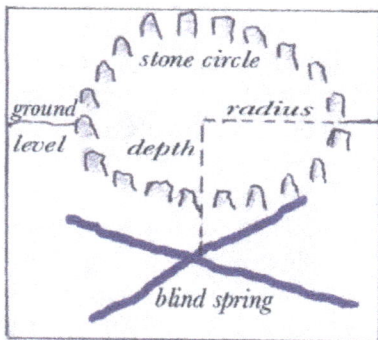

Poynder (1992) explains this energy thus :-
"Underground water has a very strong vibration therefore producing visible energy in the colour spectrum into the atmosphere above ground level. This vibration builds up into powerful spirals easily discernible with a pendulum, or in the hand of a traditional rural dowser." (page 61).

Poynder (2000) also puts forward a plausible explanation for the different shapes of stone circles as measured and presented by Thom. He claims that they come about as a result of the different shapes formed by the underground blind springs which affect the shape of the spiral sensed by prehistoric man on the surface. Thus, if the underground water courses cross at right angles, a truly circular stone circle is formed. The other most common 'circle' shapes are egg - shaped or flattened at one side - these are again affected by underground water courses. These are illustrated in the diagrams on the following page.

Other features, such as standing stones, ancient tracks, earthworks etc., all mark the energies and currents produced by underground streams, cracks, underground tunnels and fault lines. The energy courses along in tracks and spirals beneath the ground.

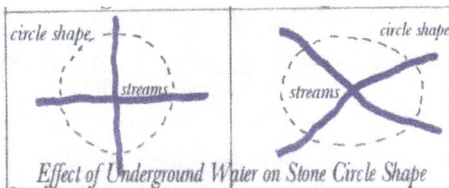

Effect of Underground Water on Stone Circle Shape

As Michell (1983) puts it :-
"The current that runs along these lines is

everywhere related to the traces of prehistoric engineering, to lines of standing stones and earth ridges. Its course, therefore, has evidently remained constant for thousands of years…"

Effectively, standing stones were placed over blind springs to control the energy spiral and flow. (see below). It is interesting to note that the concentric circles of energy at the surface exactly match the pattern produced as a result of dowsing. It is also clear that stone circles control the energies in a different way, effectively forming a boundary wall around the energy spiral, although the guided 'overground' is not bound in.

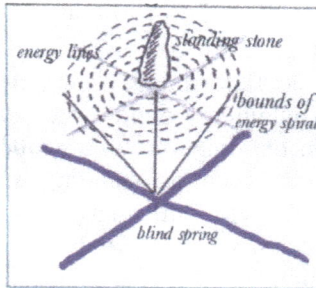

The earth currents can then be considered as a sort of grid system with the energy flowing along lines under the earth - including watercourses and fault lines. However it is also apparent that prehistoric man was able to control the flow to some extent by the use of the standing stones, circles etc.. He could , in a limited way, guide the flow to where it was required by the placing of standing stones in appropriate positions and distances from the circles. It is likely that the parallel lines of standing stones, known as avenues, may be conductors of the natural energy, as has been dowsed at the West Kennet Avenue leading to Avebury (see Chapter 7). Conversely, there is some evidence to show that it has proved possible to break up the natural energy flow by blocking it, effectively shorting it out. The Roman Catholic Church has achieved this in a number of ways at a number of sites - this is discussed in detail in Chapter 6.

Our ancient forebears did not just rely on the terrestrial energy in their daily lives but were also able to call on the power of the sun. They had the technology to draw down solar power and use it to 'top up' the energy in the underground channels. This was again achieved by using the stone circles and the monoliths. The solar energy reaches the earth as heat and electricity which is absorbed by, particularly, the circles and monoliths over the blind springs. The sun's energy brings positive electrons during the day and the reflected light of the sun from the moon brings negative electrons during the night. This changes the polarity of the underground water courses from day to night on a small scale and on a larger scale from week to week to reflect the changing patterns of the solar wind - 'the breathe of God' as it came to be known. This is caused by the rotation of the Earth on its axis and around the sun, plus magnetic variations in the sun itself.

Electricity also builds up in clouds and during storms and this is, of course, given off in the form of lightning. The circles and monoliths acted as conductors of this electricity and drew the energy down into the underground water. At times of excess energy, the surplus simply flowed back into the atmosphere. Prehistoric man, most particularly the

95

shaman/priests, used this power to assist in the growth of plants in due season, as well as for healing and for ritual purposes.

Prehistoric man was able to increase the intake of solar power and to spread the terrestrial energy on to the 'grid' by means of the materials he used in the stone circles, monoliths and mounds such as Newgrange in Ireland. The most common mineral associated with these features is quartz, and quartz is an excellent conductor of electricity. It can also generate small amounts of electricity both from the heating effects of the sun, known as pyro - electricity, and also when pressure is applied to the mineral, as happens during different phases of the sun and moon, known as piezo - electricity. Quartz takes many forms other than its most common white one, they include rock crystal (clear), amethyst, citrine, as well as rose, smoky and cairngorm. All these varieties share the power to generate a small electrical charge, used in modern times in watches and computers. Quartz is found in nearly all stone circles either in its white form, as at Newgrange and the Duloe Circle in Cornwall, or as at the Easter Aquorthies Circle in Aberdeenshire which is made up of stones of a variety of different crystals. Many circles and monoliths are made up of granitic rocks and granite is composed of three main minerals, quartz, feldspar and mica. It is therefore ideal for the purpose as quartz and feldspar are good conductors and mica is the best mineral for the storage of an electrical charge. Quartz is, of course, also known to be slightly radioactive which, according to Devereux (1999), could produce trance - like states in shamans, which would be useful for ritual purposes.

Quartz Rock at Duloe Circle in Cornwall

Another way in which the ancients contrived to enhance the energies at their disposal lay in the careful construction of the mounds, such as the ones at Newgrange and Knowth in Eire and probably too at Silbury. They were carefully constructed in a way that bears similarities to a modern battery. As Michell (1983) describes it :-

"The chamber itself is lined with stone covered with a layer of turf and with successive layers of clay and sod. These layers are carefully built up, different types and colours of clay being used at each stage. Finally the whole structure is buried under a great mound of earth." (p.89)

It is likely that, at a location such as Silbury, the build up of the energies as a result of the construction method and the materials used could be used by the shamans to assist in the growth of the crops in the surrounding area. This, of course, would emphasise the importance of the Hill as the altar to the Harvest Goddess.

Primary Leys

Having briefly studied leys and how the energy was 'topped up' by our ancestors, is there anything that might indicate some sort of national ley lines? Many researchers claim to have discovered long leys which have come to be known as 'primary leys'.These may be distinguished from true leys not just by their length, but also their width, not just being as straight and narrow as a laser beam, but varying in width more like a corridor. Michell, who had already discovered a curved ley running through Goring, Stonehenge, Glastonbury and Llantwit Major in south Wales - the latter three being locations of the so-called perpetual choirs, made the major geomantic discovery of the St. Michael Line. This is a line stretching from St.Michael's Mount in Cornwall right across the southern half of England, entering the sea near Lowestoft on the east coast. It has been called the 'dragon line' because it links a series of churches dedicated to St. Michael and St. George, both noted dragon slayers. Two further points are well worth considering, that the area around this primary ley contains the greatest concentration of dragon legends in the country and that the terrestrial energy currents are known as 'dragon currents' in many countries.

The main point about the St. Michael Line, whilst acknowledging that it is a significant feature linking ancient sites, is that it is not absolutely straight and some researchers have thought that it is, in fact, a series of interlocking leys. However two dowsers, namely Hamish Miller and Paul Broadhurst, decided to follow the energy line all the way from St. Michael's Mount to the North Sea. They followed the twists and turns of the line until, in its complex twists around the Avebury circle and henge, they realised that it crossed another line travelling broadly in the same direction. They returned to Cornwall and traced both lines as they weaved their way along the ley. The two currents became known as the St. Michael, the 'male', line and the St. Mary, the 'female', line. The two lines meet and cross at major nodal points along the ley, such as Glastonbury Tor and Avebury.

Such leys have come to be called 'caduceus' leys after the staff carried by Hermes/Mercury/ Thoth/ Asclepius (the Greek God of Healing) which has two serpents entwined around the central staff. The staff represents the backbone (e.g. the original St. Michael line) and the serpents represent the vital energies around the spine (sometimes called the kundalini energy), in other words the male and female energy lines. Where the two lines cross at the major nodal points may be considered as the chakras or psychic points along the line. Miller and Broadhurst presented their findings in their book 'The Sun and the Serpent' (1989).

Devereux and Thompson writing in 1979, before the energies had been dowsed, decided that, whilst the St. Michael line was not a true ley, it represented a wonderful piece of divination on the part of Michell and that it was a significant landscape element. They realised that it was like a wide avenue stretching across the south of England with the sites located along it - they accordingly gave the St.

99

Michael Line the title of being a 'geomantic corridor'.

Sites along the St. Michael Line 1/ St. Michael's,
Carn Brea, Penwith. 2/ St. Michael's Mount.
3/ Helston, Cornwall - patron saint = St. Michael.
4/ St. Michael's Chapel, Carn Brae, Camborne/Redruth.
5/ St. Michael's Chapel, Roche Rock, Bodmin.
6/ The Cheesewring, Bodmin Moor. 7/ St. Michael's ,
Brentor, Dartmoor. 8/ The Hurlers Stone Circle.
9/ St. Michael's, Burrowbridge Mump. 10/ St.
Michael's, Othery.
11/ St. Michael's, Glastonbury Tor. 12/ Stoke St.
Michael.
13/ Avebury - Silbury.
14/ St. George's, Ogbourne St. George. 15/ Royston
Cave.
16/ Wandlebury Stone Ring.
17/ The Abbey, Bury St. Edmunds.

Guy Ragland Philips (1976) named what he called
the Belinus Line after the legendary King Belinus (380
- 363 B.C.E.) and the line was purported to follow
one of the straight roads that he built. It is of
significance that Bel or Belinus was also the Celtic
God of the Sun, who was reborn as St. Michael with
the arrival of Christianity. Philips first traced the
line through Brigantia, the old northern kingdom of
England, passing through Congleton, Alderley Edge,
Manchester, Kirby Lonsdale and Carlisle. He later
traced the line on to Brading Villa in the Isle of
Wight in the south, via Birmingham and Winchester,
and to Inverhope on the coast of Scotland in the north,
via Pitlochry. The line has been dowsed by Gary
Biltcliffe and Yana Nilsson amongst others and

found to encompass the same male and female energy lines as the St. Michael ley. They have been called the Belinus (male) current and the Anna (female) current, after the Goddess Anu and Anna, the wife of Belinus.

It is amazing that, just as the St. Michael Line is centred on the great 'serpentine ' complex at Avebury, comprising the great circle and henge plus the Beckhampton and West Kennet avenues, so the Belinus Line is centred on Shap in the Lake District which, although they are now sadly largely destroyed, comprised similar circles and avenues. It is worth noting that the word 'serpent' has often been used in parallel with the word 'dragon' and may refer to the dragon legends and the twisting currents in the earth.

Sites along the Belinus Line 1/ Brading Villa, Isle of Wight. 2/ Titchfield Abbey.
3/ St. Catherine's Hill, Winchester. 4/ St. Mary Bourne.
5/ Highclere and other Templar sites. 6/ Seven Barrows on the Ridgeway. 7/ Uffington and Dragon Hill.
8/ The Rollright Stones.
9/ Brailes Hill and Meon Hill - sacred hilltop sites.
10/ The Bull Ring, Birmingham, a former Bronze Age temple.
11/ Shugborough Hall.
12/ Biddulph Grange, a former Rosicruci 13/ Manchester.
14/ Whalley Abbey.
15/ Casterton Circle, south of the Lake District. 16/ Shap.
17/ Long Meg and Her Daughters Stone Circle, near Penrith.

18/ Carlisle, an ancient British centre. 19/ Eskdale.
20/ Rosslyn Chapel, a Templar and Masonic site. 21/
Pitlochry, the geographic centre of Scotland. 22/ Clava
Cairns, a prehistoric centre.
23/ Culloden.
24/ Lairg, a prehistoric centre. 25/ Inverhope.

The sites along the St. Michael Line are all aligned
to the sunrise at Beltane, which is May 1st, whereas
the sites along the Belinus Line are all aligned to the
midday sun at the summer solstice, June 21st.

St. Michael Line - Examples
1/ St. Michael's Mount - south west coast of Cornwall.
This was a site sacred to the ancient people of
Cornwall who worshipped it because of its shape (see
Chapter 2) and because of its location on an
energy line. Supposedly named after a vision of St.
Michael in 495 A.D., it housed Celtic Christian monks
prior to the Norman invasion. The Benedictines built a
priory here in 1135 and it was linked to the
monastery at Mont St. Michel on the French coast,
which was the senior house of the two. It is of interest
that the little town of Marazion is nearby on the coast
of the mainland. The name is said to be a
modification of the name for a Thursday market, but
it seems more likely to refer to a Jewish market,
reflecting the number of Jewish visitors in early times,
including, it is said, Joseph of Arimathea and Jesus'
son.

2/ St. Michael's Chapel, Roche Rock, Bodmin.(see
accompanying photograph).
A large mass of granite rising out of Bodmin Moor
and topped by the small chapel, built in 1409. The

102

ancient tale attached to the Rock was that St. Cercun
of the true Celtic church was a hermit living in a
cell among the rocks in the early years of
Christianity. He became the first Bishop of Cornwall
and left to go to St. Michael's Mount. Prior to his
time, the Rock was one of the natural features
worshipped by the nomadic groups of the Neolithic
period (see Chapter 2). Just a mile from the Rock is
Roche's Holy Well (holy wells and springs will be
dealt with in greater detail in Chapter 10.).

3/ St. Michael's Church, Othery, Somerset.
The church is situated on the crest of what was an
island in the formerly flooded Somerset Levels. The
island is made of massive limestone which provided
excellent building materials. This was a place of
refuge in Neolithic times and venerated by the people
of that era. The church is a fairly ancient foundation
and it is believed that there was a foundation of
Celtic Christian monks before the church was built.

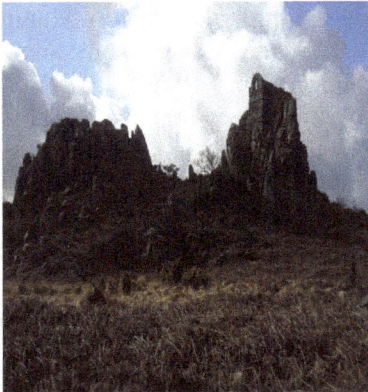

St. Michael's Chapel, Roche Rock

103

St. Michael's Church, Othery, Somerset

4/ Burrowbridge Mump (also Burrow Mump).
This is located in that part of the Somerset Levels known as Sedgemoor. It appears to have been constructed by man, so regular is its shape. It is made of a red clay, deposits of which are only found several miles away. It must have been constructed in late Neolithic or early Bronze Age times, in the same fashion as Silbury Hill. The long axis is quite clear at 27degrees north of east, which is the same alignment as Glastonbury Tor. There is a small, ruined chapel to St. Michael on its summit.

Burrowbridge Mump

5/ Glastonbury Tor.

The Tor and the town at its foot are reputed to be one of the most sacred sites in England, although this is somewhat diminished by the rampant materialism that seemingly obsesses the local inhabitants! Glastonbury Abbey and the great abbey at Bury St. Edmunds (also on the St. Michael/Mary line) were, according to John Michell (1973, page 74), "the two greatest abbeys of medieval England." Whilst it was a natural hill, formerly an island in the Somerset Levels, the hill gives the impression of having been artificially shaped to emphasise the terraces and the top. The church of St. Michael was on the summit, although only the tower now remains. The twin energy lines weave around the hill in an amazing fashion. The hill is aligned in exactly the same direction as Burrowbridge Mump, i.e. 27 degrees north of east. Further details of

105

Glastonbury and its sacred role in English history are included in Chapter 10.

St. Michael's Tower on Glastonbury Tor

The Templar, Royston Cave

6/ Royston Cave

It would seem that Royston is a more significant element on the St. Michael Line than might at first appear. The cave itself is reportedly of Medieval and Templar origin
- being supposedly cut to provide a combined two level storage room and chapel for the Knights Templar travelling from nearby Baldock to the weekly market at Royston. The walls are covered with graffiti depicting numerous figures and symbols, including St. Michael, St. Christopher (Hermes) and perhaps St. Catherine (the Christianised version of Persephone, Queen of the Underworld) carrying the wheel of fortune. There is also a depiction of a Templar knight with his hood and the cross carved on his surcoat (see above illustration).

The market town is an important geomantic site at the intersection of two straight 'Roman' (i.e. pre - Roman) roads aligned to the four cardinal points of the compass, including the well known Icknield Way. It has been speculated that Royston represents the three levels of the early world - the cave represents the underworld, the market place (the crossroads) the physical world and a maypole-like structure mounted in the still visible, but displaced, Roy Stone pointing to the upper spirit world. The cave and market town may thus be perceived as an *axis mundi* - a wonderful sacred site.

The Cheesewring, The Hurlers, Avebury and Silbury Hill are discussed elsewhere in this book.

The Belinus Line - Examples

1/ Highclere.

Highclere is a village in Hampshire that was an

107

important ritual area for the prehistoric people. There are numerous tumuli in the district. In the late eleventh century, the land was ceded to a member of the St. Clair (Sinclair) family, at least six of whom travelled over with their kinsman William the Conqueror and were duly rewarded for their aid. The castle built at this time was called High Clere (one of the many variant spellings of the St. Clair name. This was one of the numerous St. Clair holdings in Hampshire and the south east, including, locally, Burghclere. The castle was rebuilt twice, latterly in the nineteenth century, when it became the home of the Carnarvon family of Valley of the Kings fame.

The inherent sacredness of the site and the proximity of the energies of the Belinus line must have contributed to the desire of important people to live there.

2/ The Uffington area.

Whilst not on the grand scale of Avebury, Stonehenge or Callanish, the Uffington complex is an important spiritual area in its own right. It comprises the Uffington White Horse, the hill fort and Dragon Hill, with Wayland's Smithy only a short distance away along the Ridgeway. The White Horse is probably the oldest in the country, although its actual age has been long disputed. Many people have suggested that it is Anglo-Saxon in age, but it is generally agreed now that the Horse is late Bronze Age to Iron Age in date. There has also been a long dispute as to what is actually depicted in the carving - a horse or a dragon! Many archaeologists have suggested that it was a tribute to Epona, the horse goddess of the Belgae, the local Celtic people. Others

108

have suggested that it was a depiction of the dragon that St. George reputedly killed on Dragon Hill, which is located just below the figure. Yet others have maintained that the carving is of St. George's horse. Suffice it to say that the carving does look more like a horse, but then it is possible that the scoured out figure has been modified in the past 3,000 years to suit different tastes.

Dragon Hill is fascinating to look at from higher up the slope (see following photograph). It has a bare patch on the summit where the blood of the dragon was reputedly spilt and the legend has it that nothing will ever grow there. On the day the author and friends visited there was a light haze over the bare patch, visible on the photograph, which, given the day, could not be explained as heat haze.

The hill fort, Uffington Castle, is probably of Iron Age date with the classic banks and ditches, probably with timbers around the top and perhaps a facing of local sarsen stones. Whilst some researchers claim that this place is the location of Badon Hill, where King Arthur defeated the Saxon invaders, there is little evidence to support this.

3/ The Rollright Stones.
This famous circle in Oxfordshire has recently been taken over and developed by the Rollright Trust. Access has been improved and land purchased enabling this wonderfully atmospheric circle to be seen to better advantage. The circle is part of a small complex of three monuments - the King's Men (the circle), the King (a single marker stone) and the Three Knights (a cove setting a couple of hundred metres away). These names are derived from a legend ascribed to the

area in an attempt to frighten the local people away from it (see Chapter 6).

Dragon Hill from the Uffington White Horse

The Rollright Circle from the portalled Entrance

The energies associated with the circle are phenomenal, with many of the stones emitting a pulsing energy, the taller stone on the right of the above photograph is a good example. In addition the dowsed energies across the circle are very pronounced with no less than eight concentric bands between the edge and the centre. Enthusiasts should seek further details in 'Places of Power' by Paul Devereux and on the Rollright Trust website.

4/Arbor Low Henge and Circle.
This is a very important site in Derbyshire and has been called 'the Stonehenge of the North' because of its comparable significance to Stonehenge. The henge is a high bank encompassing a partially filled-in ditch. Within the ditch, there is a flat plateau-like surface with a circle of recumbent stones. In the centre of it all there is a four stone setting which is probably the remains of a cove. Some discussion has taken place as to whether the stones were originally placed upright and have since been blown over by the strong winds that blow across this open country. In favour of this argument is the fact that a few stones are not absolutely flat on the ground, but, as against this, no evidence of 'socket holes' for the stones has been discovered, and the great majority of the stones appear 'in situ'. Aubrey Burl is of the firm belief that the stones were originally upright ('Circles of Stone', 1999, page 16). There are two 'entrances' to the henge and circle - in the north-west and south-east, perhaps evidence of ceremonial avenues having once existed, similar to those at Avebury.

The complex seems to have been erected in late Neolithic times, perhaps 5,000 years ago and lies at the centre of eight early Neolithic chambered tombs and a large number of mid to late Bronze Age barrows. The whole effect therefore is of a sacred landscape dedicated to death and fertility and the ancestors - over a period of probably two thousand years. This again illustrates a similarity with Avebury and a uniformity of religious practice across the country. One of the later barrows is actually incorporated into the henge bank and another, Gib Hill (named for being the site of a gibbet in the Middle Ages), the largest, is only a few yards away to the south.

This is undoubtedly an important sacred site and seems to be a 'link' between the sites at Avebury and Stonehenge and the other major complexes at Shap and the great stone circles of the Lake District. The terrestrial energies are quite strong at the site, particularly centred on the central cove which appears to be aligned to the major northern moonrise to the N.E. The site is also said to be the focus of no fewer than fifty leys, but this issue is complicated by the large number of other monuments in the vicinity which may have given rise to accidental alignments.

Arbor Low.

Showing the bank, ditch, recumbent stones and central cove. The partially standing stone is visible at left upper centre. Photograph taken from the barrow.

5/ Shap

There are signs that this area must have been a significant sacred complex in Neolithic and Bronze Age times. Sadly though it has suffered even worse desecration than Avebury. The lonely remaining stones of the Kemp Howe circle decimated by the construction of the west coast main railway line, the surviving stones of the avenue going north to Shap village and the ploughed out remains of Skellaw Hill (the Hill of the Skulls) are all that remain.

The Remains of Kemp Howe Stone Circle

5/ Long Meg and her Daughters.

This is one of the great Cumbrian circles and it has plenty of atmosphere and energy. The circle is large, measuring about 110 metres from west to east and 94 metres from north to south. It is slightly flattened on the northern side and aerial photography has revealed that it was constructed against some form of enclosure, which accounted for the flattening. There seems to be a portalled entrance in the

S.W. with perhaps lesser entrances to the west and east. The heavily carved, sandstone pillar of Long Meg stands aloof, some thirty metres beyond the S.W. entrance and has been aligned to the midwinter sunset. Long Meg has numerous symbols carved into its inner surface, facing the circle, including spirals, concentric circles and cup and ring marks. It has been suggested that these carvings may relate to its astronomical function.

Long Meg, N.W. Face

6/ Rosslyn Chapel.

This amazing sacred site was known to tens of thousands even before the publication of 'The Da Vinci Code'. The building was commenced in 1446 by William Sinclair and was never completed. Despite being started almost 150 years after the so-called elimination of the Knights Templar, it is full of Templar symbolism, including the floriated cross, the lamb carrying a banner (Agnus Dei), the five pointed star, the dove bearing an olive branch and the stylised Head of Christ (known as the Veil of Veronica or the Mandylion).

As well as the Templars, the Chapel is also sacred to the Freemasons - the organisation that grew out of the Templars and most of the symbols in the chapel are important to the masons too.

The Chapel has been described as 'an arcana in stone' and was built by William Sinclair on the principles of sacred geometry and is said to match the ground plan of the Temple of Solomon. Stonemasons were brought in from the Continent and were housed in the specially built village of Roslin - they were said to be members of the guild known as the Children of Solomon, which had links to the Templars.

Two of the main carvings in the Chapel are linked - the lintel bearing the famous 'omnia vincit veritas' inscription (truth conquers all) and the adjoining Apprentice Pillar which is supposed to represent the Tree of Life, linking Heaven, Earth and Hell. At the foot of the Tree, the Dragons of Neifelheim (of Norse mythology) are gnawing at the roots, preventing the fruits of Knowledge from growing on the tree. The combined carvings form a wonderful spiritual message.

Other symbolism in the chapel includes over one hundred 'green men' peering out from the carved foliage, probably representing the cycle of birth and rebirth, vegetation indigenous to North America (fifty years before Columbus discovered that continent) proving that another Henry Sinclair had sailed there fifty years earlier. The whole building seems to carry information about ancient, sacred knowledge for 'those with eyes to see.'

With regards to the energies of the site, as well

as being on the Belinus Line, Rosslyn is the focus of a number of true leys and, unsurprisingly, Rosslyn Glen, bordering the Chapel and Castle grounds was settled in ancient times. A couple of miles from Rosslyn lies the ancient preceptory of the Templars in Scotland - Balantradoch, now known as Temple - with its atmospheric ruined church and graveyard, with assorted Templar and Masonic gravestones.

Rosslyn Chapel

The Old Templar Church and Preceptory Site, Temple

7/ Bulnaraun of Clava.

These have become known as the Clava Cairns after a type of burial site found in this part of Scotland. These cairns, unlike the large chambered cairns found elsewhere in the country, discussed in Chapter 8, are smaller and seem to have been dedicated to the memory of members of the ruling elite of the tribe. The monument consists of three fairly small cairns comprising a circle of kerbstones, with the central area infilled with a large number of water worn pebbles and boulders. Around each cairn there is a stone circle. Each cairn has a central burial chamber with the two outer ones having a passageway leading to this chamber. In each case, the passage is aligned to the south west and the setting sun at midwinter. This alignment is also reflected in the kerbstones which are graded to the

S.W., the largest stones facing this direction. The more colourful stones also face this direction. Some of the stones were carved with cup and ring marks before they were put in place (see Chapter 11). This is a wonderfully atmospheric site, fittingly sited on this important geomantic line, as is the nearby battlefield of Culloden.

Chapter Six
Short Circuiting the System

Short Circuit :- 1.to cause a short circuit in (so as to render inoperable); 2. To bypass or circumvent.
Longman's Concise English Dictionary, p. 1279.

Truly it has been suggested that history has been written by the victors. The advent of the Bronze and Iron Ages saw the development of male aggression and the weapons to go with it. This in turn led to the Roman occupation of much of the country and it is the history of this period that is generally considered important enough to have been taught in schools until comparatively recently. In modern times, new products and forms of power are produced and then misused to develop weapons of war - just as the manufacture of iron was soon used to produce swords, spears etc., over 2,500 years ago.

The spiritual power emanating from the stone circles and monuments has gradually waned because of the diminishing spiritual nature of the people, but the real change came with the Roman invasion and then the advent of Roman Catholic Christianity. Here we had an empire and later a religion but ultimately they both had the same goals - power and domination.

The Romans hated the Druids, the Celtic priests who had done so much to maintain some spiritual authority in the country, despite the constant warring between tribal factions. As well as this hatred, the Romans could also see that the ancient spiritual sites in the landscape of Britain were focal points for resistance to their invasion and control. They therefore set out to diminish the authority of these sites. It is amazing how many of these ancient sites are either bisected by the straight Roman roads or at least have them running close to them. It is well to remember that many of these roads were pre - Roman in origin but that the Romans put a hard, metalled surface on them for speed of movement.

As Cope states (p.136) :-

"The Romans now made severe plans for sacred places of ancient influence such as megalithic monuments, which they recognised as potential political powder kegs which must be policed thoroughly."

The aim of the Romans was to have the roads run so close to the ancient sites that troops from the nearest fort could reach centres of dissent as rapidly as possible to quell any potential uprising. Thus the major 'pagan' centre at Badbury Rings in Dorset was made the crossing point of two Roman roads, including Ackling Dyke. The same Ackling Dyke went within two kilometres of Knowlton Henge and actually broke the magnificent Dorset Cursus and on to Maiden Castle. Another road totally disrupted the Avebury area, aiming at Silbury Hill, past the Sanctuary and along the Kennet Valley past the Marlborough Downs. In Yorkshire, where there are numerous ancient sites, the Romans constructed Dene Street to control the Brigantes tribe and also another road across the Wolds to control the tribes living in the sacred complex around Rudston and the Gypsey Race.

However these tactics by the Roman army should be seen as mainly political and military rather than an attack on the spiritual beliefs of the people, already in disarray following the final elimination of the Druids on Anglesey (see Chapter Eight).

However the intervention of the Christian church was a totally different matter. The rapidly growing Roman Catholic Church was noted for being ruthless in its search for power. As Cope puts it (ibid, page 139) :- " But when the Emperor (Julian the Apostate, supporter of the Mithraic religion) met an untimely death at war in Persia in 363 CE, the elders of the Christian Church regained power and vowed that usurpers such as Mithras would never again wrestle control from them. And, as Colin Wilson writes, the Christian Church 'proceeded to oppress with an efficiency that Nero would have envied'".

It is interesting to note that this oppression has been continued by varying means and by a variety of Christian sects for the following 1,642 years - as evidenced by the concerted attacks on the novel by Dan Brown, 'The Da Vinci Code', an attempt to put forward some alternative historical facts against the background of an adventure story.

However the attacks on the sacred landscape of Britain from at least the time of the Synod of Whitby in 664 A.D. until the twentieth century were far more physical than verbal, indeed they would have constituted a violation of the human rights of people in modern times.

In 601 A.D., Pope Gregory saw that overt attacks on the sacred sites were proving counter-productive and sent the following message to Mellitus, the Archbishop of Britain :-

".... the temples of the idols should on no account be destroyed.

The idols are to be destroyed, but the temples themselves should be aspurged with holy water (purified), altars set up in them and relics deposited there.... In this way we hope that the people, seeing their temples are not destroyed, will leave their idolatry and yet continue to frequent the places as formerly, so coming to know and revere the true God."

The Church in Britain used a wide variety of interesting ways to follow the instructions of Pope Gregory and we will examine exactly how they achieved their objective, with numerous examples. It should be remembered at the outset that the destruction of the effectiveness of the sacred landscape can be achieved not just be 'christianising' the monuments but also by blocking off the flow of energy to and from the monuments.

Perhaps the simplest way of attempting to win over the local inhabitants was in the Christianisation of standing stones by way of adding decoration to them - usually in the form of Celtic or other crosses or by adding Celtic Christian decoration to them. Examples of this can be found in North Wales at Maen Achwyfaen (Flintshire) and in the churchyard at Gwytherin (Conwy).

Maen Achwyfaen

In many cases, stone circles were converted into churchyards with churches placed in the middle. Very often the stones have largely been lost during this exercise - but many examples have come to light with stones built into the walls of the churchyards or set as entrance posts to the churchyard. Obviously, evidence of such a process may be seen in the occurrence of circular churchyards - although these have occasionally been extended in the intervening time to 'hide' the original form. Examples of such misuse of our ancient heritage can be found particularly in N.E. Wales, but also in mid-Wales and N. Cumbria. Particularly good examples in Wales include Efenechtyd, Tremeirchion, Cilcain and Llanarmon-yn-ial (see accompanying photograph).

**St. Garmon's Church, Llanarmon, on its raised,
circular mound**

Often the standing stones erected by the Neolithic
people to celebrate their Goddess and the 'eternal
feminine' had their power largely negated by having a
church erected right next to them - a strong echo of
Pope Gregory's exhortation in 601. Perhaps the most
famous example of this is to be found in Rudston in
North Yorkshire, where the tallest standing stone in
the country (7.5 metres) is literally right next to the
Norman church. Another example is to be found at
Gwytherin in Conwy, North Wales, where a line of
four stones are right next to the church. The church
and the stones are located on an obviously sacred
ancient mound. In addition one of the stones has been
'christianised' by the addition of a name as a
memorial (see Plate 4). The fact that both these
examples are situated on raised mounds perhaps

125

betrays that their spiritual use went beyond the erection of the stones.

Sometimes ancient monuments, such as henges, were so large that the Church actually built their places of worship inside them with plenty of room to spare! This would be true in the case of a large henge monument or hill fort. Classic examples of this include Knowlton Henge and Old Sarum, the latter actually having a cathedral constructed inside it. It could be claimed that, in the case of Old Sarum, the fort was so large that the whole town was constructed inside it but nevertheless the cathedral was constructed to block the energy of an important ley line.

The Rudston Monolith

Gwytherin Churchyard

The Old Cathedral, Old Sarum

The Norman Church, Knowlton Henge

Knowlton, however, is a very special case. Here there is a large complex of Neolithic monuments with two henges, numerous earthworks and barrows - one of the great sacred areas of the Neolithic period in Britain. The largest henge actually has a farm inside it and is largely destroyed. On the other hand, the second henge is largely undisturbed and there are still quite powerful energies in evidence. It was in the middle of this henge that a small, solid Norman church was built. This had the double purpose of taking over the religious function of the monument in the eyes of the people and, importantly, reducing the energies focussed on the henge by sending the energy into the atmosphere. A further point is that the masonry of the church is so solid that it could well have been derived from former standing stones within the henge (much as happened at Avebury). We visited the site on an extremely wet day - in fact the rain only ceased during the one hour we were on site. The henge is astonishingly atmospheric despite the presence of the little Norman church, and the dowsed energies were amazing. As we approached through any of the entrances, a strong energy signal was received and as the church was approached no less than eight concentric energy rings were registered, but, within three metres of the church, the dowsing rods actually reversed, pointing back across the henge. Standing within the church ruins, an impression was gained of a dome of 'non-energy' encircling and covering the church. The erection of the building had clearly disrupted the ancient power by short circuiting the energy flow (see accompanying photograph. More details on Knowlton are included in Appendix A - Dowsing.).

Occasionally the Roman Catholic church achieved the disruption of the natural energies of an ancient sacred site by 'cutting through' the main energy line leading to or from the site. At Stanton Drew, this was achieved by placing the church astride the energy line linking the Great Circle and the Cove. This energy line can be dowsed, although somewhat weakened, close to the circle but is not in evidence at the Cove (the accompanying map shows the relationship of the church with the complex; a photograph of the Cove, in the grounds of the local inn, follows). Rodney Castleden (The Stonehenge People, Routledge, 1990) says about Stanton Drew :-

"Unfortunately, the medieval church has been built right beside the Cove and blocks its sight line to the two northern circles, probably in an attempt to seal up whatever pagan power still resided in the monument." (p.148)

129

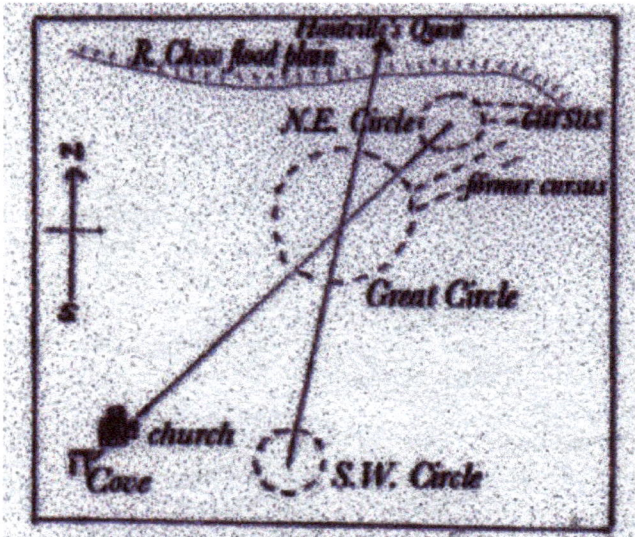

The Stanton Drew Complex

Something similar seems to have happened at the Hill of Tara, the great monument in Eire. Michael Poynder (1992) makes his feelings abundantly clear about the effect of the Roman Catholic church on this site :- "....... in order to cut Tara off from its energy, 'the curse' took the form of a Christian stone being raised at the corner of the tiny, original Christian church within the present graveyard and right over the inflow energy.

Stanton Drew Cove

By doing this, the priest effectively put in a barrier; just as if we had put a large boulder in the middle of a stream, the water is disrupted and has to part and flow around it. Tara was therefore effectively immobilised as a sacred site and after that its effectiveness as a place of magical power was lost. This was a deliberate act of energy manipulation performed with full knowledge of its effects and the history of Ireland has been predictable since, as the country has suffered ever after" (p.121-122) Strong and thought provoking words indeed!

Whilst many would disagree with Poynder's sentiments expressed in the above quotation, there is no doubt that, despite the magnificence of the sacred site, there is an absolute absence of energies and atmosphere on the hilltop. There is a feeling of desolation and desecration making it a sad place to visit.

131

The religious bigotry that was fomented in the Middle Ages later led to the diminution or destruction of many of the wonderful spiritual sites that were erected by our ancient ancestors. We have alluded in previous chapters to how many references to our ancient past were subsumed into the new Christian religion, such as prominent dates within the so-called 'pagan' calendar, or names from the old 'Goddess' culture being used in a derogatory sense (covered in some detail in Chapter 2). In Chapter 3 we commented on the destruction of many of the triple Goddess settings of standing stones as late as the seventeenth century - showing how vestiges of the old beliefs must have survived in some aspects.

The full extent of this paranoia and desire for power can only be realised by a study of the myths and legends with the stones and other sites down to the present day. The full effect that these stories must have had through to the eighteenth century must be set against the belief patterns and education of the mass of the people - whipped up by the pulpit orators of the day. The majority of the populace became too scared to approach many of the ancient sites for fear of what holy wrath might descend on them.

It should be remembered that the ancient sites possessed telluric (earth) energies, because of their location on the energy lines, often 'topped up' by solar energy taken into through the quartz-based stones. However the energies were also increased by the human energy of the people involved in the rituals that took place there - the chants, prayers and dances all took their part in this reaction (remember the example of Rede Church mentioned in Chapter 5). The result of the constant efforts of the priests to turn the people away from their 'pagan' ways has been the gradual diminution of the power of the stones over the centuries - although some sites such as Men-an-tol in Cornwall have been used right up to modern times by adults seeking healing for their children, of attempting to conceive, even by farmers clinching deals by the clasping of hands through the 'quoit'.

There follows an outline of the legends that have been attached to twelve sites mentioned in other chapters in this book.

1/ Swinside Stone Circle or Sunkenkirk (Cumbria).
The legend here is that the people were attempting to build a new church in the valley on this site. Each night the Devil came and removed all the stones that had been erected. The stone circle is supposed to represent the remaining foundations of the abandoned church. Similar tales are found elsewhere in the country.

2/ Long Meg and Her Daughters (Cumbria).
Long Meg (the isolated monolith) was supposedly a witch and the stone circle her daughters. They were turned to stone by the priests for practising witchcraft. Interestingly enough, when attempts were made to destroy the circle in the eighteenth century, a huge thunderstorm arose, thus ending the attempt.

3/ Rollright Stones (Oxfordshire).
This is a combination of a circle (the King's Men), a monolith (the King) and a dolmen (the Whispering Knights). They were petrified by a witch due to the greed of the King wanting to rule over all of England. The witch said that if he could see the

133

nearby village in six huge strides, she would grant his wish. He failed and he and his army were immediately petrified. It is interesting that Paul Devereux (1990, 1999) has identified that the road running through the site is a 'spook' road along which strange sightings have occurred.

4/ Stanton Drew Circles and Cove (Somerset).
The circles are petrified wedding guests and the avenues (see previous map) are the fiddlers. They were encouraged to dance past midnight on a Saturday by the Devil and were therefore turned to stone for dancing on the Sabbath. The Cove is made up by the petrified forms of the bride and groom, with the drunken priest lying on his back!

5/ The Hurlers (Cornwall).
Here the stones are the petrified figures of a group of young men who were playing the game of hurling on the Sabbath (note that this Sabbath story is a recurring theme around the country).

6/ The Merry Maidens (Cornwall).
The stones are the merry maidens who were happily enjoying themselves dancing on the Sabbath and therefore petrified. The nearby two stone setting, known as The Pipers, were playing the music for the maidens to dance to.

7/ Callanish (Isle of Lewis).
A race of giants inhabited the island and were strongly resistant to being converted to Christianity and were turned to stone for their sin by St. Kieran.

8/ Silbury Hill (Wiltshire).
The Devil was carrying an apron full of earth to deposit on the inhabitants of nearby Marlborough. He was prevented from doing this by the priests, whose power forced him to drop his load near the River Kennet.

9/ The Rudston Monolith (N. Yorkshire).
The Devil threw a huge stone like a spear at the church, but such was the power of the local priest that the stone was diverted and landed by the church.

10/ Willy Howe (N. Yorkshire).
This large, imposing barrow not far from Rudston was reputedly the home of fairies who would entice unwary travellers to partake of food and drink which, once consumed, kept them there forever.

Willy Howe

11/ The Devil's Arrows (N. Yorkshire).

The Devil fired these arrows (three now but probably four or five originally) at the little town of Boroughbridge, but they were diverted by the priests and fell to earth here. Cope, in 'The Modern Antiquarian' states that the area between the rivers Swale and Ure is sacred and was dedicated to the goddess Ur.

The Devil's Arrows

12/ Men-an-tol (Cornwall)

The 'holed stone' or quoit was once part of a stone circle. Children could be healed of their ailments, including rickets by being passd through the hole nine times against the sun. The priests called the stone the 'Devil's Eye', hoping that the threat of the evil eye would keep the people away.

Most of these tales illustrate a particularly

muscular Christianity and seemingly an unforgiving God, at least as portrayed by the priests of the time!

Men an Tol

The Roman Catholic church also either capitalised on, or diminished, the natural energies of ancient sites by giving them a Christian 'makeover'. This fact has been covered in greater detail in Chapters 2 and 10, the first outlining the denigration of the goddess figures by defamatory use of their names and the latter by way of providing the principal wells and springs with suitably Christian legends.

When all else failed the answer to the problem was the actual destruction of the ancient sites. It has been said that Stonehenge suffered great destruction in Roman times. Avebury underwent severe depredation in the seventeenth and eighteenth centuries, mainly at the instigation of the Protestant church, when the local farmers were persuaded through bigotry and religious intolerance to destroy the stones. Many were used to build the houses in the village - indeed ghostly happenings are still reported in some of the houses! There are numerous tales of workmen being killed whilst destroying the stones and indeed a skeleton has been discovered crushed beneath one of the toppled Avebury megaliths. It was common practice to fell the stones and then to break them up by building huge fires around them. Archaeologists working on the stones of the Beckhampton Avenue have discovered evidence of fires in and around the former stone holes. There are also numerous tales of tremendous storms, with thunder and lightning, occurring when people have attempted to destroy the circles, such as the one already mentioned at Long Meg in the eighteenth century - so dramatic that no one has dared to try and destroy it again!.

One can only wonder at the destruction that has occurred to our wonderful heritage during the past two thousand years in the frantic scramble to eliminate the 'eternal feminine' and replace it with the masculine oriented Christian religion - the replacement of spiritual energy with what is effectively temporal power. Fortunately, enough of the ancient energy remains to provide the 'Islands of Light' with the impetus to move forward to a new spiritual age.

Chapter Seven
A Complex Situation

Within the overall sacred landscape that makes up a great deal of Britain and Ireland, there are areas that form distinct ritual centres where the living came to revere, and commune with, their ancestors and to worship their gods. In such places the 'genius loci' is almost tangible, even four thousand years or more later, in a far more material world. The earth energies at such places are still clearly evident when dowsed. It is also true to say that these places were sometimes centres of 'pilgrimage' into medieval times, often being particularly attractive to the Knights Templar, and they are increasingly attracting modern seekers after spiritual enlightenment.

Such ritual complexes include the environs of Stonehenge, Avebury, Arbor Low in Derbyshire, Kilmartin Valley in Argyllshire, Callanish in the Hebrides, the Yorkshire Wolds (the area around the Rudston monolith) and the Boyne Valley in Ireland. Many of these ancient landscapes are but shadows of their former exciting selves - we would cite the area around Arbor Low and that in the Yorkshire Wolds in this respect. However others can be identified as retaining much ot their former glory. It is proposed to examine two of these in more detail to see just how integrated these landscapes are - namely the Kilmartin Valley in Scotland and the area around Avebury in Wiltshire.

The Kilmartin Valley

The Kilmartin Glen in Argyll may perhaps be distinguished as the sacred area with the greatest variety of ancient sites encompassed in such a small area and with such a spread of time periods. The heart of the glen is no more than three kilometres by two kilometres and the whole ritual area is about twelve kilometres by five. Sites range from the early Neolithic through to the Templars and beyond - roughly five and a half thousand years.

The uses of the sites vary from the rock carvings at e.g.Dunchraigaig, burials along the valley floor, stone circles in Temple Wood, cists in the same location, henges, barrows, evidence of worship around water (see Chapter Ten), the coronation stone of the early kings (Dunadd), early Celtic Christian crosses, through to Templar burials in Kilmartin churchyard and others locally, as well as sundry forts, duns, castles and crannogs.

The importance of Kilmartin Glen as a religious complex is illustrated by the way in which the sites from different ages are 'layered' on top of one another - this can be compared to the way in which the chambered tomb of Bryn Celli Ddu in Anglesey (Chapter Nine) has been built on top of a previous henge monument. In Kilmartin, this has been carried out on a fairly large scale, emphasising its significance as a part of the true sacred landscape of

140

Britain.

There is evidence, in the valley, of standing stones being located in relation to the surrounding landscape to observe sun, moon and stars, probably for calendrical and astronomical reasons. Many of the burial sites appear to have been used for ritual and celebratory purposes as well as burials. The question of petroglyphs (rock carved symbols) is covered in greater detail in Chapter Eleven, but the fact remains that the concentration of cup-and-ring marks and spirals located in this region is greater than anywhere else in Great Britain, even compared to the east Pennines.

This seems to further illustrate the argument that once certain points in the landscape are perceived and designated as 'sacred', they remain so to successive generations often for thousands of years. It is perhaps the case that a location, having achieved 'sacredness', remains so for ever - despite the prevailing mores of the day. In the case of Kilmartin, it would appear that the whole glen was deemed sacred, with certain points showing up as particular foci for reverence.

Rachel Butler in her informative guide "Kilmartin" has this to say :-

"The stone circle at Temple Wood and the circular enclosure at Ballymeanoch henge had been special places in the landscape for many generations. Hundreds of years after their construction, people placed burial kists in both monuments."

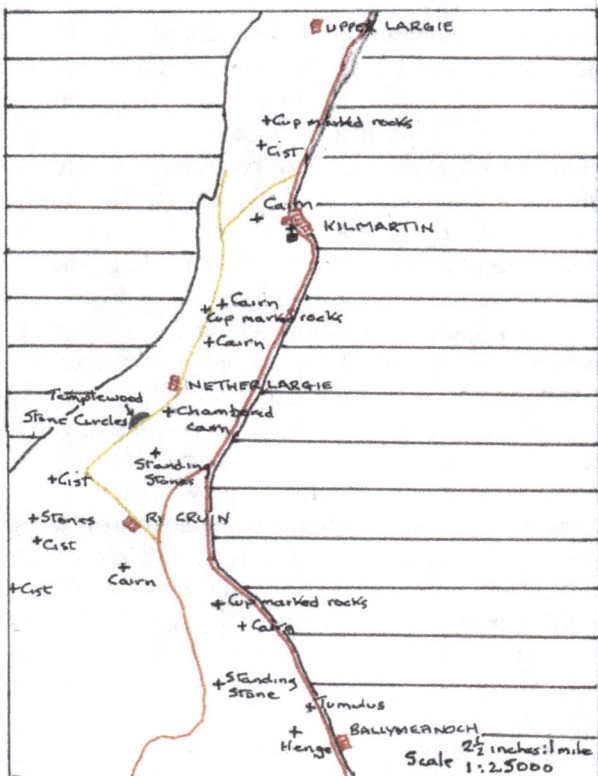

The Main Ancient Sites of Kilmartin Glen

They placed their dead in places which were already recognised for their antiquity and spiritual power." (page 62.)

And "Whatever motivated its evolution, Kilmartin's landscape communicated an overwhelming sense of power - the power of the architects, of the past on which they built, of the

142

universe to which the monuments referred, and of the monuments themselves.

This power was both spiritual and political, and its maintenance may have seemed crucial to the continued existence of life in the valley." (page 56.)

An important point to remember when looking at the Valley is that nowadays we see but a remnant of what was there even two hundred years ago. The remaining cairns in the linear cemetery have been much damaged when the land was cleared for the plough in the nineteenth century. There were also many Neolithic monuments on the gravel terraces that flank the valley floor along much of its length.

It is most important to reiterate that, such is the sacredness of the sites in Kilmartin, many have been used and reused time and again from about 3,500 B.C.E., thereby accruing more and more sacredness in the eyes of the people as generation gave way to generation.

1/ Templewood Stone Circles.

There are two circles evident within Temple Wood (this name itself may be a reference to the advent of the Knights Templar in the fourteenth century). The smaller, northern circle was commenced in about 3,500 B.C.E. as a timber monument, later to be replaced with stones. It was perhaps a solar observatory. The larger, southern circle was commenced in about 3,000 B.C.E., with a stone setting. The whole Templewood complex was in use for about 2,000 years and contained many kist burials. The southern circle with one of its kists is shown on one of the following photographs. There is evidence of carvings on a few of the megaliths -referred to further in Chapter11. The circles are highlighted by the use of river washed pebbles in their construction, perhaps bearing comparison with Swinside and Mayburgh henge. Altogether, this skilfully reconstructed site is extremely atmospheric and still carries the 'feel' of spirituality - one can gain a sense of the rituals that must have taken place here.

2/ The Ballymeanoch Henge.

This is one of the very few henge monuments in Scotland and sadly is in a ruinous state, having largely been ploughed out.

Templewood Stone Circle

Templewood Stone Circle with Kist

Originally constructed about five thousand years ago, it had two entrances, one to the north and one to the south. Whilst there is no evidence extant as to its former usage, it must be surmised that it was used for ritual gatherings of the local inhabitants, much as in the rest of Britain. What is known is that, hundreds of years later, from about 2,000 B.C.E. the henge was used for a number of interments.

3/ Nether Largie South chambered cairn (see following photograph).
This is the only chambered cairn in the area, dating back to about 3,000 B.C.E. The cairn was carefully constructed to include a stone built chamber for the storage of human bones over several generations. Whilst the remnants form a round cairn, many archaeologists consider that it was probably

originally a long cairn, similar in style to West Kennet and Wayland's Smithy, 'rounded off'much later, in about 2,000 B.C.E. to match up with the rest of the cemetery. At this later time it seems to have been used for many kist burials and there is a surviving kist at one end of the cairn.

The monument still preserves a tremendous atmosphere and emits a powerful, pulsating energy that may affect the traveller.

4/ The Linear Cemetery.
The other four cairns in the 'cemetery' were constructed in the early Bronze Age, between 2000 -1500 B.C.E. They are simple mounds with no internal chambers and contain many kist burials. The most southerly cairn, Ri Cruin (the Kings' Circle), has some unusual carvings associated with the kists - including carved axe heads and another carving, involving a long line with short strokes off it. This latter carving has defied interpretation but does appear like an early version of the Ogham script and may be a form of proto - writing.

The fact that there is a series of five cairns along the valley floor in a line stresses the significance that this area must have had to numerous generations of Neolithic and Bronze Age people. It was clearly an important component of their spiritual life and their belief in the importance of the ancestors and the continuity of life.

Paul Devereux in his book, 'The Sacred Place' (2000) comments on the significance of the alignment of cairns, which are spread over some three kilometres in a south-west to north-east direction.

"Obviously, the people buried in the cairns must

have been important to the society that constructed the monuments, and it is reasonable to assume that they were great leaders of some sort, but we should bear in mind that the role of such leaders could also have incorporated religious functions, making them priest-kings or shaman-chieftains. This is especially so as a strong tradition of sacral kingship existed in Scotland during pagan Celtic times ...." (page 157)

This latter statement is particularly interesting in the light of similar traditions existing in Egypt and the Middle East in the same period, continuing through to Jesus the Christ, and the line of the Fisher Kings and the Merovingians in the Europe of the so-called Dark Ages.

5/ Nether Largie Stones.
"Two pairs of stones with settings of four or five stones in between" (Kilmartin, page 92).

The precise dating of these stones is difficult but it seems that the megaliths have been in position for about 5,000 years. Many observers,seeing this unusual setting for the first time, instinctively believe that they form part of some sort of observatory. Some archaeologists have suggested that they were used in conjunction with the Temple Wood circle.

Nether Largie Cairn

Nether Largie Standing Stones

Hadingham in his book 'Circles and Standing Stones' (1976, p.124) discusses the relevance of the Nether Largie Stones and Temple Wood for lunar observations. He states:-

"Temple Wood (including the stones) could have operated as a self-contained observatory, with all the facilities necessary to observe both maximum and minimum limits of the moon about every nine years, and this unusual combination of sight lines may account for the highly distinctive layout of the site"

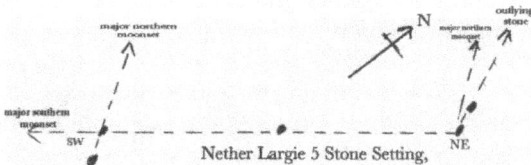

Nether Largie 5 Stone Setting,

Devereux, in his previously mentioned and excellent book 'The Sacred Place', shows that the stones can be intimately related to the major north and south moonsets, illustrated in the above diagram adapted from his book. It may be considered highly unlikely that these alignments are merely fortuitous.

A further point that seems significant is that most of the stones contain cup marks which 'echo the direction of the long moonset alignment' (ibid, p.140).The central stone of the group contains no less than 40 cup marks, which may therefore represent lunar symbolism.

6/ The cup and ring marks.

The megaliths and rock surfaces of Kilmartin Glen are famous for the cup and ring marks, and the sheer variety of symbols within that overall definition. This is probably the greatest concentration of such carvings in Britain, exceeding even the Yorkshire Pennines and the Boyne Valley in Eire. The greatest assemblage of the symbols is to be found at Baluachraig, Dunchraigaig, Kilmichael Glassary and Ormaig, Cairnbaan and Achnabreck further to the south of the area. These tend all to be placed on fairly horizontal surfaces as opposed to those on the Nether Largie Stones (above). Some suggested meanings for these carvings are suggested in Chapter 11.

Visiting these sites in Kilmartin Glen, one cannot fail to be moved by the message that the ancestors were trying to pass on to succeeding generations.

7/ Dunchraigaig and Ballymeanoch Cairns.

These are situated towards the south end of the valley. Dunchraigaig is located on a river terrace and contains a wide variety of burials, including single burials and a number of cists containing both cremated ashes and un burnt bones. Ballymeanoch has been almost 'quarried out' but evidence remains that it was a ring cairn with kerb stones and was probably built later than the other monuments in the valley - about 1300 B.C.E.

8/ The sacred pool and associated features.

These have been recently excavated on a gravel terrace near the head of Kilmartin Glen, as reported in 'British Archaeology Now' in April, 2002.

Dating back to c.2000 B.C.E., archaeologists have discovered a large peat filled hollow, seven metres wide and two metres deep, which was thought to have been a sacred pool, surrounded by an inner ring of posts, possibly totem poles. Around this was an outer ring of thirty oak posts, forming a circle

150

roughly forty-seven metres in diameter. From this circle a timber way or avenue led down off the terrace on to the valley floor.

Traces of burials were evident linked to this monument - a cremation burial under a stone at the foot of one of the totem poles and six cist burials in and around the circle.

Yet again these early Bronze Age structures were placed on earlier sacred sites - most notably the end of a Neolithic cursus or processional way, some 45 metres wide and constructed of close set oak poles. There are also charcoal remnants from a Mesolithic campsite some 6500 years old.

9/ Dunadd.

This rocky hill is located in the south of the area, just to the south of the little river Add. It really emphasises the sacredness of the area in the eyes of the local people and beyond. This place was tremendously important to the Scoti tribe who arrived from Ireland in the fifth century A.D. The rock surfaces at the top of the hill are decorated with carvings including a boar and an inscription in the early Irish ogham script. There is also a rock cut basin and carved footprint believed to be associated with the ceremonies surrounding the inauguration of the early Scottish kings between the sixth and the tenth centuries A.D.

10/ The Templars.

There are some sixteen churchyards, both ruined and still in use, in the area, that have grave slabs that seem to be clearly associated with the Templars. Most notably these include Kilmartin, Kilmory and

Kilneuair churchyards. The fact that many Templars came to Scotland after the dissolution of the Order is now accepted by most historians and the presence of so many graves in this one small area would tend to show that these 'holy warriors' recognised the inherent sanctity of the valley.

Let us leave the last word on the wonderful Kilmartin Glen complex to Rachel Butter in her 'Kilmartin' guide to the valley - she adopts a spiritual approach to the interpretation of this magnificent prehistoric landscape.

"Hundreds of years after their construction, people placed burial kists in both monuments (Temple Wood and Ballymeanoch).

They placed their dead in places which were already recognised for their antiquity and spiritual power.

Similarly the linear cemeteries were built on old foundations.

When people built round cairns on top of the older structures, and added others - all in a line - they unified the landscape. The space between became as important as the monuments themselves. The Valley was now dominated by one composite monument, and the whole landscape expressed the power and importance of its architects." (page 62).

I believe that this sacredness and unity of landscape is what defines the great prehistoric complexes of these islands. Be they on the western isles of Scotland or the chalk downlands of Wiltshire, these sites are an evocation of the spirituality of the people and the natural sanctity of the landscape. I propose to examine this further in a consideration of the cohesive landscape that is Avebury.

Avebury.

The area around Avebury in Wiltshire is undoubtedly one of the most studied parts of the British Isles, archaeologically speaking. Although the area is larger and less clearly defined than the Kilmartin Glen, there is a tremendous concentration of monuments and a definite cohesiveness to the landscape. One feels that this area is trying to say more to us about Neolithic and Bronze Age beliefs than Kilmartin, which simply presents a unified landscape. Around Avebury the various sites seem to be inexorably linked one to the other - the only question we have to ask, and struggle to answer is 'how?'. It is proposed to look briefly at the interpretation of this magnificent sacred landscape and to seek out points of interaction between the different sites, and then to move on and look at some of them individually.

Francis Pryor in his book 'Britain B.C.' bases his interpretation around the work of Mike Parker-Pearson, of Sheffield University, and Ramilisonina, from Madagascar. Based on their work and his own insights, he sees the monumental landscape as being about the relationship between the living and the dead and the gradual transition between the one and the other.

He writes, on page 191, of the Neolithic attitude to death as follows :-

"Death to us is almost always a tragedy. But to many non-Western societies, death is as much a beginning as an end. Of course people in prehistory felt grief, loss, pain and emptiness; but there was hope too, and in the longer term there was the prospect of transformed existence and renewal. Life

153

and death, like the seasons themselves, formed part of a continuum."

Pryor perceives that the sacred landscape around Avebury evolved between about 3,500 B.C.E. and the start of the Bronze Age, roughly 2,000 B.C.E. He postulates that, at the beginning of this period, the area in the S.E. of the following map - round the Sanctuary - was the Domain of the Living, whereas the area to the west, from Windmill Hill southwards was the Domain of the Ancestors and that the Avebury circle as it then was was between the living and the ancestors. By the end of the Neolithic, the fully completed Avebury Circle had become the focus of the Domain of the Ancestors, the northern area had become, as he calls it, the Liminal Zone (the barely perceptible or sensory zone) of early Bronze Age burials, the area to the west (with Silbury Hill now fully operational) was between the living and the ancestors and the area to the south was the Zone of the Living, with focal points at the ceremonial circles flanking the river Kennet.

It is proposed that the local inhabitants would gather in these circles - then probably move on to the Sanctuary - maybe along the river Kennet (as probably happened at Stonehenge with the people moving from Durrington Walls and Woodhenge along the river Avon) - and, following the necessary rituals, process along the West Kennet Avenue with the bodies of the dead to the two inner circles at Avebury. The recent discovery and excavation of the remains of the Beckhampton Avenue would seem to indicate that something similar took place from this side of Avebury. There is even the possibility (unproven thus far) that two further avenues

154

approached Avebury from the north and the east - which would demonstrate even further the magnificent significance of the great circles as a ritual centre for a large area.

Pryor's concept stresses the great importance of the ancestors to our ancient predecessors and of the relationship between the living and the dead. It is about the afterlife, rebirth and renewal.

Michael Dames, on the other hand, in his work 'The Avebury Cycle' (1977) sees the great complex built into the Avebury landscape as a direct reference to the Goddess and the ancients' worship of her. He believes that the Stone Age farmer saw the whole landscape in terms of representations of the human figure and, even more, built his sacred monuments to emphasise this fact. Thus the landscape around Avebury is conceived as the figure squatting as for childbirth.

As Dames puts it (ibid, page 186) :-

"What the landscape around the Kennet headwaters provided was a particularly vivid, medium-scale version of this Mother Earth reality, inspiring a particularly vivid architectural response. No fewer than twenty seven monuments of the fourth millennium B.C. (including Windmill Hill camp) were arranged around the periphery of this topographical squatting goddess image, in order to define it more clearly."

To Dames, the west-east chalk escarpment overlooking the Vale of Pewsey provided the arms, head and neck of the goddess, the buttocks around Windmill Hill and the area around the West Kennet long barrow and a ploughed out site, known as G.55, provided the groin and the vaginal area.

The adjacent Silbury Hill, Dames sees as the pregnant Harvest Goddess. The great causewayed enclosure of Windmill Hill, as previously mentioned, according to Dames provided part of the buttocks of the goddess and, interestingly enough, there are a large number of ancient pits on the Hill which also produce the shape of the crouching pregnant goddess, according to the same author. His illustration of the 'Pit Goddess' is reproduced below.

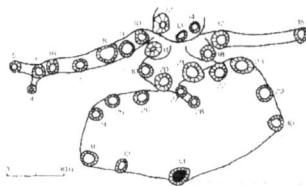

The pit goddess.

Whilst freely admitting that the people of the Neolithic saw anthropomorphic representation in the landscape, as discussed in Chapter 3, it is difficult to envisage that they would have been able to 'see' the outline of the goddess like a 'dot map' on an undulating landscape, building their sites on the outline. For instance, the spread of the arms would have been in the region of eight miles and the distance from the outstretched left hand to the feet about ten miles.

Dames sees the Avebury complex as a cycle in worship of the goddess with the focus at Silbury Hill, where the goddess gave birth to the harvest child - just as the harvest has become celebrated throughout the centuries into modern times. But the whole

Avebury cycle was a celebration of the goddess in all her aspects – it was an annual series of celebration by our Neolithic ancestors.

As Dames has it (ibid, page 217) :-

"Silbury, Sanctuary, the avenues, and the Avebury henge, collectively possess the concentrated energy of a microcosm, epitomising the Great Goddess as she turns through her annual gyrations. What a stroke of genius it was to encourage the outward flow of this force through bringing the inner monumental image-world into contact with the composite goddess at the West Kennet barrow. Acting as tomb to the inner circle and vulva to the more diffuse outer figure, the barrow raised the life and death opposites into happy accord."

Dames devotes considerable time and energy in developing his thesis of the Avebury Cycle and it is impossible to give it full coverage a work of this nature but certainly his focus on goddess worship and the 'death' part of the Cycle focussed at West Kennet pick out the salient features of Neolithic spirituality - namely birth, death and rebirth - leading inevitably to the worship of the great Mother/Goddess - hinged around ceremonies based on the avenues and the Avebury circle and also Silbury Hill.

Paul Devereux is undoubtedly one of the outstanding writers on all aspects of sacred sites and their spiritual significance. He has studied the Avebury complex in some detail and eventually reached the conclusion that the final focus of the area was Silbury Hill, built between 2,700 and 2,600 B.C.E. He realised that the Hill had been constructed so as to be visible from all the other major monuments of the area. It can be seen from the principal long barrows of the district, also from Windmill Hill, Avebury Henge and the Sanctuary. It seems to have been constructed with a low platform to reach a height similar to the surrounding land - and to be just visible from the above landmarks.

The platform, some five metres below the summit of Silbury Hill, permits Windmill Hill, one of the great really ancient sites at 3,700 B.C.E., to be visible from the extended east end of West Kennet, another of the most ancient sites (see Chapter Eight). Observation from all the principal sites showed that in all cases the background landscape was shown between the summit and the ledge - this cannot be coincidental in so many cases.

The construction of Silbury Hill was commenced in early August, as evidenced by the bodies of flying ants being found in grass in the turf that forms the core of the mound. As Devereux points out, this is the time of harvest and cereals were known to have been grown in this area at that time. This may be seen as evidence that Silbury was representative of the harvest Goddess - "suggesting that it was connected with harvest celebration and rituals - the forerunners of Lugnasa and Lammas (Celtic harvest rituals) - and the fecundity of the earth in general."

(Devereux, 'The Sacred Place', p.163).

He also sees another purpose for the platform on Silbury Hill in that the sun always rises in the same place at the spring and autumn equinoxes - from the summit of the Hill, looking east, the sun rises over the distant horizon and, if one then drops down to the platform, the sun appears to rise again over the nearby Waden Hill.

Devereux therefore concludes :-

158

"Interpretation is always a risky business, but it seems reasonable to see Silbury Hill in terms of acting as an intermediary between the fecundity of the Earth and the source of life, the sun - considered to be a Goddess, Sunna, in early northern Europe. Perhaps the great mound symbolised the Earth Mother herself." (ibid, p.164).

He sees that the goddess worship can also be carried through to the symbolism of the great stones at Avebury, with the so-called 'Vulva Stone', the diamond shapes of many of the stones, and also names such as the Kennet river, formerly the Cunnit, with its sexual symbolism.

In summary then, whilst Pryor tends to focus on the relationship between the living and the dead, in death and rebirth, in his analysis of the ritual landscape of Avebury, the other two authors, Dames and Devereux, take a balanced view between the life/death aspect and the worship of the Goddess. They see, as did, I believe, Neolithic man, that these are two aspects of a composite whole. We will now go on to look at some features of the Avebury complex not studied in detail elsewhere in this book.

1/ West Kennet Long Barrow.

This feature is looked at further in Chapter 8 - but it is the oldest extant feature in the Avebury landscape, being in use from about 3,800 B.C.E.. As described, it was modified at least twice at later dates, including the blockage of the entrance in 3,300 B.C.E. Many of the barrows and mounds in this area do not seem to have been used for burials which tends to indicate that they must have been used for rituals, probably connected with death and the passage to the afterlife.

2/ Windmill Hill.

Located in the north-west of the area, this is the second oldest site in the complex, with a triple ditch causewayed enclosure constructed in about 3,700 B.C.E. This date was arrived at by analysis of the domestic rubbish in the bottom of the ditches. Whilst Dames believes that the thirty-two pits around the top of the hill were dug at this time and the ditches somewhat later, most archaeologists concur that they were contemporaneous. This site can be seen from all around and the glowing white of the bare chalk when it was first constructed must have been wonderful to see.

It is generally agreed that Windmill Hill was not the location of permanent dwellings, but was perhaps at best seasonal. It was most likely reserved as a special place for festivities and celebrations and, no doubt, rituals. It could be seen for miles around and must have been a magnet for the local community and beyond at such times.

It seems that in this early period of the Neolithic, the focus of the life of the people lay in the west of the area, with the people living lower on the river terraces and celebrating life and the harvest at places such a Windmill Hill and death at West Kennet.

3/ Avebury Henge and Stone Circle.

Avebury was built between 2,900 - 2,600 B.C.E. It is likely that that the henge was built first, cut into the chalk. The ditch was at one time 10 metres deep and the combined depth of the ditch and embankment must have been about 17 metres. The diameter of the henge, between banks, is about 427 metres.

Within this henge, a huge stone circle was constructed, with over 100 huge stones, sarsens from the nearby downs. Unfortunately, due to the destruction carried out by local residents mainly in the eighteenth century encouraged by 'Mother Church', only 27 of these stones remain in situ. The rest were broken up by fire and hammers and used in the construction of the village. There are two smaller circles within the large one with few stones remaining, the southern one has 5 stones out of 29 and the northern one 2 out of 27. The small southern circle used to contain the Obelisk, probably the largest stone in the complex, which was destroyed, and it is interesting to note that the local people used to dance around the maypole in this circle until the nineteenth century. The northern one contained the Cove, a three sided feature of huge stones used for ritual purposes.

In its full magnificence, the main circle with its internal 'temples' must have been wondrous to see with the huge 100 stone circle surrounded by the glowing white ditches - what worship and rituals must have taken place here! As can be seen on the accompanying map (see following page), even with their limited numbers, the stones of the main circle are still energised and linked. This was evidenced by dowsing the entrance and between two of the other stones (see Appendix A for Dowsing). The energy would undoubtedly have been far stronger 4,500 years ago given the complete circle of stones and the greater spirituality of the people.

It is interesting to note that nowadays the great circle is famed for the amount of spirit activity that is reported. This is particularly around the stones and in a

161

number of the nearest houses, strangely enough those built from blocks of stone from the megaliths broken up in the last four hundred years!

4/ The Avenues (see following map and photographs). There is clear evidence of two avenues, one leading to the south entrance of the circle and one to the west. The former, the West Kennet Avenue is still clearly seen extending about 2.25 kilometres from the Sanctuary to Avebury. Only 27 of the original 100 stones remain, but concrete marker posts indicate many of the rest. The stones alternate between wide 'diamond' shapes (female) and tall, thinner ones (male).

Two quotes illustrate the wonderful feelings elicited by walking in the Avenue.

One from the Internet (ancient.ways/avebury) :- "Walking along the West Kennet avenue towards Avebury is the best way to approach the stone circle. You can feel emotions with each footstep of all the people that have taken this route over the past 4,500 years."

One from personal contact with an elderly German lady in the middle of the Avenue, talking of the stones in the Avenue she said :-

"They are all individuals in their own right, I wish I could understand their meaning."

To walk along the Avenue towards the Circle is an awe-inspiring experience. The deliberate changes of direction, each one marked by broken pottery and bones placed at the foot of the stones, the rising anticipation as one comes closer to the Circle and then the final turn (on a compass bearing of due North) which is where one actually catches sight of the massive entrance stones. One can mentally and

162

spiritually picture a procession coming along the Avenue to be greeted by the priest/shamans at the entrance.

The energy was dowsed at three locations along the Avenue (two of these represented on the following map). The results were the same in each case. The stones forming the periphery of the Avenue are linked by bands of energy - the dowsing rods cross as one moves across the boundary. In the centre of the 15 metre wide avenue, the dowsing rods move parallel to each other, indicating a noteworthy current of energy flowing along the Avenue towards the Circle.

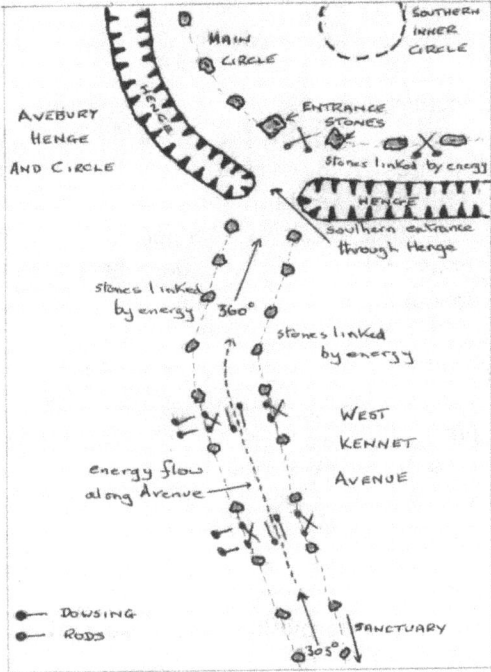

The Beckhampton Avenue, arriving from west of the Circle and again about 2.25 kilometres in length, was first described by William Stukeley, that great explorer of ancient monuments, in 1724. So much destruction of the stones took place after he wrote of them that people in modern times actually doubted the existence of the avenue - but recent excavations by teams from Southampton, Leicester, Newport and Newcastle Universities have revealed that the Beckhampton Avenue must have been every bit as impressive as the West Kennet Avenue. Well might Stukeley write about how "a few miserable farmers destroyed this, the noblest of monuments which is probably on the face of the earth"!

(Stukeley, 'Abury Described,1747).

5/ The Sanctuary.

At the opposite end of the West Kennet Avenue, 2.25 kilometres from Avebury, lies the Sanctuary on Overton Hill. This was built before Avebury as a timber structure. A stone circle was added at the same time as the construction of Avenue. There has been much speculation about the purpose of the Sanctuary but it seems likely that it was both a mortuary temple and a place where rituals could take place prior to a procession along the Avenue to the Circle. Nearby there were enclosures where people would have lived. It seems likely that there would have been a similar set up at the far end of the Beckhampton Avenue.

6/ Silbury Hill.

Further to the information provided earlier in the chapter, the Hill is some 37 metres high and the summit is about 30 metres across. The hill was built in three stages between about 2,700 and 2,200 B.C.E.. Stage 1 was about 20 metres across and surrounded by a wattle fence. This flat central area had a clay mound covered in earth and turf. Earth and stones were then piled on top of this to produce a mound 5.4 metres high and about 36 metres across. Stage 2 took place in about 2600 B.C.E. and involved building the hill up with chalk to about 73 metres across. Stage 3 saw this greatly increased to about 178 metres across. This was built up in a series of steps, made of chalk quarried from the area around the mound - giving rise to the effect of an island standing within a lake. The steps were then filled in with chalk rubble and earth.

It is possible that Silbury Hill was not only built as a site marker in the complex and as a harvest goddess, but that it had been deliberately constructed as an 'energy accumulator' with layers of clay and turf within the chalk walls - much as in the manner discussed in Chapter 5.

All - in - all, the Avebury area forms a most wonderful unified, and unifying, complex - the sacred landscape seems to have strong cohesion. The area has the oldest causewayed camp in Europe, the oldest chambered cairn, the largest henge in Europe and the biggest man - made hill. One can only guess at the spiritual significance of this landscape to the local people to cause the erection of these monuments over a period of 1500 years. It is interesting and significant to consider the fact that, after the wanton destruction that took place between the seventeenth and late nineteenth centuries, interest in the history and intense spirituality of this landscape has reawakened gradually through the twentieth and into the twenty - first centuries.

It is a profound truth that Grace Cooke, the great medium attached to the White Eagle Lodge, and her husband, Ivan, writing in 'The Light in Britain' (White Eagle Publishing Trust) 'saw', without the aid of archaeologists, the importance of Silbury Hill as a harvest centre and the importance of the whole complex to the worship of the Mother Goddess.

"Rightly did the Ancient Wisdom incorporate the mother as its symbol of worship and also wisely because the same forms of worship will surely return, bringing in their train both peace and plenty. It is right that womanhood as a whole should be housekeeper entrusted with the earth's bounty; and the womb of the mother as the receptacle of life itself, created by love, has played at least as important a part in the affairs of mankind as has the male's over - eager intellect." (page 48).

166

Chapter Eight
"And Death Shall Have No Dominion."
Dylan Thomas

It is extremely difficult to be definitive about the nature of the beliefs and rituals of our ancestors in the pre-Christian era in the absence of any written record. Archaeologists have tended to highlight the difficulties of interpretation and have also been fairly quick to denigrate any attempts to put Neolithic and Bronze Age religious practices into perspective. However, in recent years, a new generation has started to be prepared to analyse what they see on and in the ground intuitively - and no more so than in considering the ancient attitudes to death. This work has involved the study of the remains, a detailed analysis of what were previously considered to be simply tombs and the symbols that have been carved, or, rarely, painted (in Britain), on the stones.

It is fair to say that the ancient hunter/gatherers of the Mesolithic and early Neolithic periods, more than six thousand years ago, were dependent on nature for their existence - for the animals that they hunted, the wild grasses and fruits that they gathered, the water that they drank and the caves in which they sheltered. However, from the start of the Neolithic period, animals were being gradually domesticated, seeds were being gathered and sown and hut circles were being constructed near to good water sources. Man was starting to live in a state of interdependence with nature. This in time brought about a change in the fundamental relationship between man and his gods and goddesses. People realised that they were interfering with the forces of nature, but at the same time living in tune with those same laws.Hence care had to be taken to propitiate the god(desse)s of trees, springs etc. and the idea of ritualistic worship started to develop. It was at this time that settlements such as Grimspound and that on Holy Island in Anglesey evolved. Man realised that the Sun God was crucially important for the growth of crops and therefore for continued existence. Hence the masculine solar god came into prominence.

Man obviously realised early that dead bodies had to be dealt with in some way, rather than leaving them littering the landscape to be picked over by the crows. Quite clearly, burial in one form or another was the only viable option. As Bord and Bord state (1986) :- "There is evidence of human burial in the earliest prehistoric times, the Old and Middle Stone Ages, but the first tombs date from the New Stone (Neolithic) Age, after 4000 B.C.. These tombs are oldest prehistoric monuments to survive in Britain…. There is no doubt that great care was taken in housing the dead, and that over the centuries many thousands of tombs, some very elaborate, were constructed in Britain and Ireland." (page 27).

Prior to the Neolithic, it would appear that bodies were left in the open air, perhaps on some form of platform, until they had either decomposed or been

168

picked clean until they became skeletons and then the bones would have been gathered together and stacked on ledges in caves with the skull placed on top. This seems to have continued into the Neolithic except that tombs were now constructed to house the skeletal remains, often in separate side chambers, although this may have been for important members of the tribe with lesser members being left to decompose in the old way. The construction of these tombs varied from area to area and these variations will be discussed later in the chapter. Later the bones were often buried in cists, small stone 'chests' in a ritual setting (as at Woodhenge or at the Templewood stone circle in Argyll). Cremation was also an option and, dating from the Iron Age, burials are often discovered with the ashes placed in earthenware vessels.

The important aspects of the burials lie not in the burials *per se* but in the rituals and beliefs that might have developed around them. Evidence has been gathered that seems to indicate that our ancestors did not view death as the final act in life's drama. They seem to have believed in an afterlife and probably reincarnation and these beliefs were linked up with the cycle of nature - of death (winter) and rebirth (spring). It is also probable that fertility and sex were involved in these beliefs.

"Although there are no written records telling us what our ancestors thought about death, or whether they believed in an afterlife, there are some tantalising hints that they did not accept death as final. ... Apart from such practical considerations as providing the dead with food and drink, there is also some evidence that prehistoric man believed that the pattern of life, death and rebirth was linked to the rhythm of the sun and moon…" (Bord and Bord, ibid, page 29).

Similar to the custom in Egypt, our ancestors provided bowls of food and drink for the dead, for their journey into the afterlife. It seems clear that Neolithic man and later the Celts believed that the life and death replicated the forces of nature and their worship was arranged around the pattern of the seasons with light, warmth and water in the Spring bringing about the rebirth of the crops, and the belief that spirits of the dead were reborn into babies. They apparently did not believe, as do the Christians, that 'at the last trump' the dead will rise up and bring about 'a new heaven and a new earth'. This seems evident in the fact that the ancients disarticulated the skeletons, often stacking different bones from different bodies in different piles. The skulls of the dead, for instance, were often kept separately from the body bones. It is also likely that the tribal shamans regarded the skulls of the ancestors as oracles for the tribe, to be accessed when the shaman was in a trance state. This could be seen as calling on the wisdom of the ancestors - ancestor worship seems to have been a vital part of the pre-Christian religion. The bones of the dead were often placed in tombs, such as Newgrange in Ireland or the Wessex long barrows, at the time of the winter solstice, when they believed that the spirit would gain easier access to the spirit world as the veil between this world and the spirit world would be at its thinnest at this time. It was at this time of the year too that the tribe prayed for the weather to be clement in the coming spring and for the fertility of the crops and the increase of the tribe.

There is some evidence that the structures which incorporated burials varied in their usage over time and area - individual examples will be discussed later in the chapter. Many structures were concerned with burials alone, or perhaps rather with death. Castleden writes of this obsession with death in the sense that the bodies went through a couple of rituals and the bones could be reused for later rituals.

"It was not so much the dead that interested the Stonehenge people (as Castleden refers to Neolithic man in Britain) as death itself, and we can see emerging an elaborate pattern of ceremonial activity based on a continuing interaction with the forces of life and death." (ibid, page 157).

Later mounds in the Bronze and Iron Ages, such as the tumuli and round barrows, were probably solely concerned with burial and death. However, very clearly, other funerary sites, particularly from the Neolithic, were concerned with rather more than just funeral rites.

Two further quotes from Castleden emphasise this (page 189) :-

"A few long barrows seem to have no human remains in them at all. They are dedicatory monuments, places where the dark forces of the universe could be confronted,propitiated,befriended; places where the polarities of life and death, decay and renewal, mysteriously joined and were converted into one another.

They fulfilled, in other words, the role of churches and temples." (my italics).

And "The chambered tombs acted as a social foci in the highland zone.

In the lowland zone causewayed enclosures and

henges met this need, but there was a dearth of enclosures of this type in the highlands. The forecourts of the chambered tombs thus take on new roles as meeting-places for discussion and feasting, as well as for ceremonies."

An example of the forecourt of a long barrow tomb, that of Wayland's Smithy, is shown on the following page.

Evidence from the likes of Newgrange and Maes Howe, discussed in further detail later in the chapter, seems to emphasise the ancients' belief in death and rebirth linked with the winter solstice, when the sun reaches its lowest point in the sky at the shortest day and commenced its long climb to its summer maximum. The so-called roof boxes over the entrance to these monuments allowed the sun to shine down the main passageway on the shortest day, lighting up the far end. It has been said that, at that time, the veil between this world and the spirit world is at its thinnest, and the spirits of the dead were enabled to pass through more easily. Stonehenge, the ultimate gateway between the two worlds, experienced a similar phenomenon at the winter solstice, and this time was obviously a focus for rituals at all such sites.

The Forecourt at Wayland's Smithy.

Paul Devereux (2001) and a team of researchers have done much to highlight the significance of ritual at many Neolithic and Bronze Age sites. They have measured the acoustics at a wide range of places and established that they were constructed to be acoustically suitable for male voices and indeed the amplification of those voices over a specifically constructed area. The megaliths have been specifically placed to act as baffles or to throw back their voices within the body of the monument. In this way the ancient monuments can be directly linked in their function to cathedrals and churches - used for religious services, including funerals and also as repositories for the dead (although less so nowadays)), but clearly having more than the single function.

The experiment at Easter Aquorthies stone circle in Aberdeenshire, as reported in Devereux (2001), was

173

conducted by Watson and Keating of Reading University. They set up an amplifier and digital audio tape recorder within the 'alcove' formed by the recumbent stone and its two flanking uprights. The conclusion that they reached was as follows :-

"The survey confirmed that the distribution of stronger sound was distinctly and almost precisely contained within the ring of stones. Anyone outside the perimeter of the monument would have remained largely unaware of the acoustic effects within - a charmed circle." (page 96).

It seems that many ancient sites were set up acoustically like the magnificent open-air amphitheatres constructed by the Romans and Greeks, where sounds from the 'stage' could be clearly heard in all parts of the construction.

Frances Lynch, an archaeologist, made the point that sites such as Newgrange were in usage for far longer than for the 'mere' burial of the dead - not that many burials were actually placed within the structures. She has postulated that the entrance to Newgrange was blocked off and that the famous roof box had removable quartz blocking stones, to be removed and replaced on a regular basis. She wondered whether perhaps the orifice had an oracular function during its later existence. This blocking of the entrance to the tombs can be seen in very many cases, the West Kennet Long Barrow and Wayland's Smithy come to mind, and one wonders if the bodies interred within the monuments came to represent all the ancestors in the minds of the ancients. The forecourt in front of the blocking stones could then continue to be the focal point for ancestor worship and for other rituals concerned with the Goddess and the fertility of the ground and of the people.

What is very clear from all the foregoing is that the Neolithic people did not believe that death was the final act in the soul's journey. The body of the deceased returned to the earth, renewing its fertility, whereas the spirit lived on providing, initially, wisdom for the tribal or family group, relayed through the shaman (or medium), and eventually to be reborn in a new body.

Castleden realises the link to the ancient folk tales, such as those of Wales contained in the Mabinogion, and sees that they relate back to the Neolithic and Bronze Ages. He refers to the folk tales thus :-

"At the heart of many of these bizarre tales is a regeneration cycle, a story of growth, death, otherworldly journey and rebirth.

The endlessly regenerate earth passes from spring to summer to inter and back again." (page 222)

The coves found in so many stone circles, as at Avebury, are a symbolic representation of the stones to be found in the layout of many ancient tombs - they are at one time a place for the dead but also represent the female sexual orifice and the womb of the earth mother - all the elements of life are contained within it. We think back to the stones of the Triple Goddess set up opposite to the male stone in the early circles and see the clear, ongoing symbolism of growth, fertility and rebirth.

It is difficult to escape the conclusion that the so-called 'pagan' peoples of the pre-Christian era possessed a powerful spirituality and a belief system that would be the envy of most people who have dwelt for two thousand years under the rigid authority of the Christian churches, or indeed under the priest-led systems of any of the great modern religions. They clearly saw that the human spirit operated to the same natural law as the crops, the animals, the vegetation and the seasons. There was a time for birth into the physical body, a period of growth, maturity, decline and death, and then, given their belief in reincarnation, after a period rebirth into another physical body. They further believed that the spirits of the ancestors were accessible to them through the agency, or mediumship, of the shaman. This would take place with the shaman perhaps in a trance, induced perhaps by 'magic' mushrooms or other hallucinogens, or the slightly radioactive water in some of the sacred wells.

It is now proposed to look at some of the great sacred 'tombs' from around the country, not covered elsewhere in this work. There are many regional variations in form of the sites and we will look at just the main ones as outlined on the following map. Time and time again we will see that Neolithic man reused the main sacred sites for burial and other ritual purposes - thereby stressing the point that these places had a sort of inbuilt 'sacredness'.

176

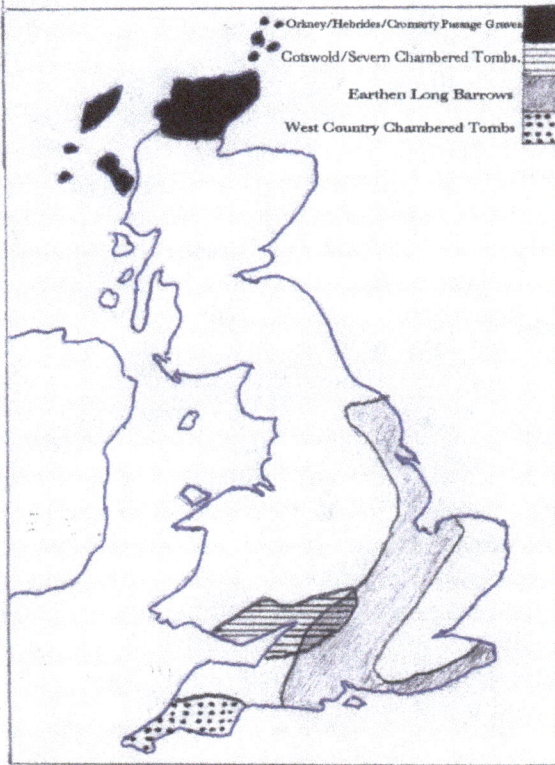

Main Types of Burial Monument

In addition, and not shown on the above map because of the general nature of their distribution, there are the portal dolmens of Cornwall and the western coastal areas of Wales and the round passage graves of Cornwall, west Wales, Anglesey and the eastern parts of Ireland.

There are clear connections between the various

forms of burial throughout the Neolithic and early Bronze Age. The round passage graves of Cornwall commenced with a simple cove - that is three or four large vertical megaliths with a heavy capstone often with a cist burial inside - the whole covered over with earth and turf. The cove gave way to a portal dolmen, the fourth side of the cove being blocked with just room to place bones or cremation ash inside, still covered over. In the intervening time the vast majority of these tombs have had the earth eroded away and we are left with the dramatic stone settings known as dolmens or cromlechs, which form such moving and atmospheric features of our sacred landscape. In a similar way the great earth barrows of the early Neolithic gradually evolved, with kerbstones to prevent collapse of the sides and then entrance facades, first in timber, then in huge stones. The culmination of this evolution were the great Severn/Cotswold chambered tombs, combining the earth long barrows and the round megalithic tombs, to be discussed shortly. Another very important point was that the later types of tomb were, almost always, erected on top of earlier monuments.

Examples.
a/ An earthen long barrow - Fussell's Lodge in Wiltshire.

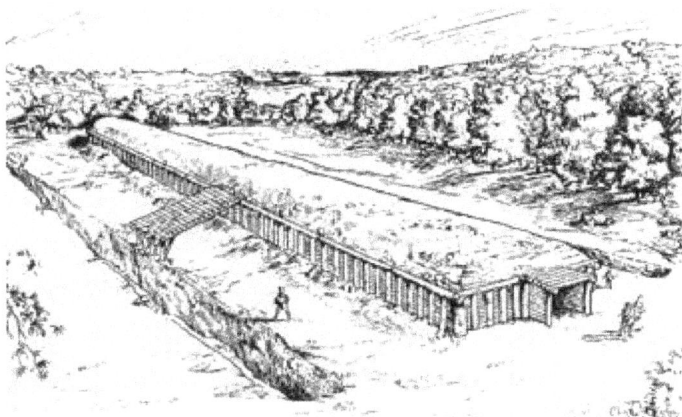

Fussell's Lodge

This was an early Neolithic long barrow with timber supports around the edge and a timber façade and entrance. It was roughly trapezoid in shape with quarry ditches parallel to the sides where the material to construct the barrow was obtained. The timber has long since rotted away and the earth barrow has been ploughed in so that only a crop mark remains to show its location. The entrance led to a mortuary room where the bones from disarticulated skeletons were stored, the bodies having been left to decompose outside for a substantial period and then the bones gathered into bundles, there would appear to have been about fifty-seven bodies interred in the Fussell's Lodge barrow. The size of the original site and the time and care that must have gone into its construction serve to emphasise the importance that these people, six thousand years ago, gave to the worship of their ancestors, and the spiritual beliefs that sustained them.

b/ A West Country chamber tomb (and cove) – Chun Quoit, Cornwall.

Chun Quoit

This is a small, simple dolmen overlooking the Atlantic and comprises four supporting stones and a 2.5 metre square capstone. The feature is about one metre high. It is surrounded by the remains of the mound including possible kerbstones. This is a dramatic and extremely atmospheric feature and the stones possess a very potent energy. Indeed Devereux (1999) has reported that the granite stones are particularly radioactive, some 123% higher than the surroundings. He also reported strange light phenomena within the setting. It is easy to picture the mound as it was and the rituals that must have taken place around it. This part of the West Country contains a plethora of sacred sites - dating back to the time when the climate was more amenable.

c. A Portal Dolmen - Trethevy Quoit, Cornwall .

This was a development of the simple passage grave described above. Here the cove had the addition of two stones acting as a portal and the tomb was more of a passage grave. One can picture the turf mound with its kerbstones and the portal with its small hole so that new bones or cremation ash could be placed inside. The dolmen stands nearly five metres high at its highest, although the dramatic tilt of the capstone was caused by the collapse of one of the uprights. This is by far the best example of a quoit in north Cornwall, given that most of the others have been destroyed in the past in the interests of agriculture and stone walling. However it is a magnificent, spirit-stirring feature in a wonderful setting.

Trethevy Quoit

As with Chun Quoit, the radioactivity is high and it has been suggested (Devereux, 1999) that the entrance is large enough to permit the passage of a person. This means that the mound would not have been used simply for burials but for ritual purposes too, perhaps with the shaman entering into an oracular trance within the setting. It is likely that the forecourt would have been large enough to permit a small number of people to participate.

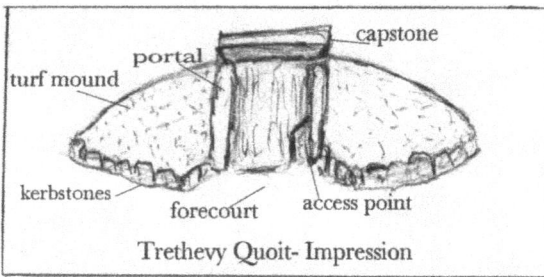

Trethevy Quoit- Impression

See also the 'twin' dolmens at Dyffryn Arddudwy, Llanbedr.

d/ Severn/Cotswold Chambered Tombs.

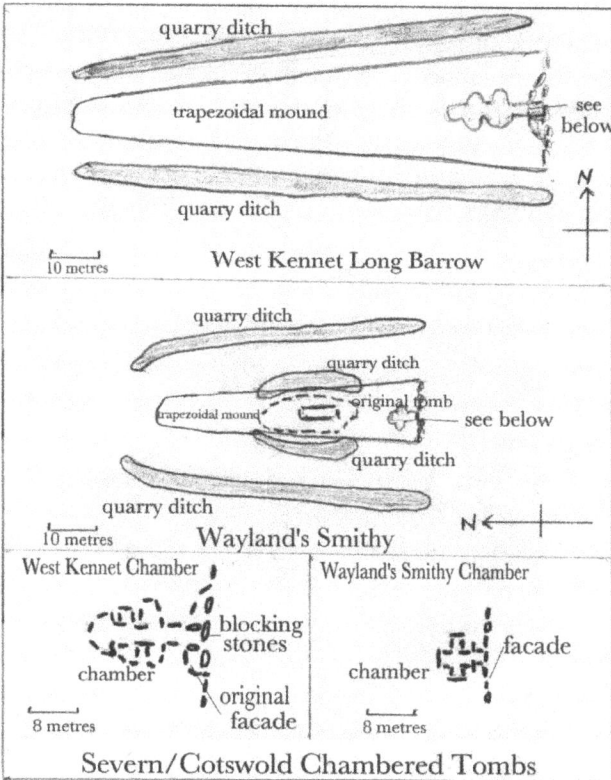

quarry ditch

trapezoidal mound

see below

N

quarry ditch

10 metres

West Kennet Long Barrow

quarry ditch

quarry ditch

original tomb

trapezoidal mound

see below

quarry ditch

quarry ditch

10 metres

Wayland's Smithy

N

West Kennet Chamber

Wayland's Smithy Chamber

blocking stones

chamber

facade

chamber

original facade

8 metres

8 metres

Severn/Cotswold Chambered Tombs

The Severn/Cotswold tombs represent the combination of two styles of tomb building - the round megalithic tombs and the earthen long barrows. It is proposed to look in more detail at West Kennet and Wayland's Smithy as prime examples of this form of monument.

West Kennet Long Barrow (see above and accompanying photograph).

This was constructed in about 3600 BCE and remained in use for over a thousand years. The barrow is about one hundred metres long and the chamber extends about twenty metres into the eastern, wider end. The site has the classic trapezoid shape and showed the 'horns' effect at the wide end, prior to the erection of the blocking stones. The material for the barrow was obtained by digging out two quarry ditches parallel to the sides.

West Kennet Long Barrow

Wayland's Smithy - Entrance

The chamber itself comprises two pairs of side 'rooms' and one at the end facing the entrance. These were all built of large stones. The chamber contained the disarticulated remains of at least 46 bodies, missing many of the skulls and long bones. This seems to show that the ritualistic habit of removing some of the bones at intervals and transporting them around the locality dates back at least five thousand years. When the site fell out of use, the so-called Beaker people filled the chamber completely with earth and stones, containing many bits of bone and ash, causing the archaeologist, Stuart Piggott, to surmise that the infill had come from a local mortuary temple.

The forecourt of the monument, between the 'horns' would have been used for ritual activity and, even following the placing of the huge blocking stones, the area in front would have still been available. The site was in a prominent location on a chalk ridge, within the sacred Avebury area and overlooking the magnificent man-made Silbury Hill and the river Kennet, or Cunnit (see Chapter Seven for further detail).

Visitors to the site have commented on the feelings of peace and tranquillity that surrounded them, the intense cold within the chamber and the gentle pulsating vibration from the stones. An impression of processions taking place to the barrow, many of them by torchlight, was also obtained.

Wayland's Smithy. (see accompanying photograph). This was constructed in about 3700 BCE, a little earlier than West Kennet. A timber long barrow was erected at that time, followed by the second, bigger monument in 3400 which was stone and earth construction.

The original barrow was perhaps twenty metres long and contained a wooden mortuary house which was paved and had two large posts at each end. It contained one crouched burial and the disarticulated remains of fourteen other people. Two quarry ditches provided the material for the barrow. The second monument, built over the first, was 55 metres long, trapezoidal in shape, with a stone built cruciform chamber and forecourt at the southern end. The remains of seven adults and a child were found within in 1919.

The barrow itself was made of material quarried from long ditches running parallel to it on either side. The mound slopes gradually upwards from the north to the front in the south. The kerbstones, used to prevent the erosion and collapse of the mound, are still in place.

Wayland's Smithy was named by the Saxons, some four thousand years after it was constructed, after their god of blacksmithing, with a legend concerning the shoeing of a horse if a small silver coin was left as an offering. The place, situated close to the chalk Ridgeway, is not in such a prominent location as West Kennet but many feel that it is the more atmospheric of the two, set within its fairly modern grove of trees - perhaps they are the successors of some original grove? The façade and chamber have a welcoming, although very cold 'feel' about them. The megaliths have a powerful energy emanating from them, so much so that one feels drawn to the site as one approaches along the Ridgeway.

e/ Orkneys/Hebrides/Cromarty Passage Tombs.

Maes Howe is a magnificent structure and a wonderful testament to Neolithic engineering. The tomb is over 7 metres high and 35 metres across and is surrounded by a bank and ditch, effectively forming a henge. It was built on a specially cut and levelled platform. It may be distinguished from a chambered tomb by the long entrance passageway, similar to those at Newgrange and other similar sites. As discussed in Chapter Four, the passageway is aligned on the midwinter sunset and this in turn aligns with two other monoliths and the Ring of Brodgar. Here we are more interested in the construction of the monument than its other purposes. The passageway is 9 metres long and is beautifully constructed of flagstone and this opens out into a chamber, 4.6 metres by 4.6 metres and about 4 metres high. There are buttresses in the four corners and huge slabs supporting the magnificent corbelled roof, a true masterpiece of engineering. Leading off from this central chamber are an end chamber and two side chambers, with entrances to them situated roughly at chest level. These were originally provided with blocking stones which are still there, on the floor of the main room. At the outside entrance to the passageway, there is a skilfully constructed recess, still retaining its original blocking stone. Maes Howe was undoubtedly built to last and so it has, for five thousand years, despite the depredations of Vikings, who left their graffiti on the interior walls, crusaders and clumsy archaeologists in the nineteenth century. The Norse graffiti includes runes, three figures, a dragon, walrus, fish and knotted serpent. Unfortunately, the depredations of the Vikings meant that the original contents of the end and side chambers had been removed, save for one fragment of a human skull. However it is thought that this great monument dates back at least five and a half thousand years. Similar to the cases we studied in Chapter Seven, Maes Howe can only be looked at in the context of the surrounding landscape. As Julian Cope states in 'The Modern Antiquarian' ;-

"Clustered around the southern shores of the Loch of Harray, on the Orkney mainland, are three of the largest monuments in Britain, which, combined with other lesser monuments, once created a landscape temple which stretched in a great arc three miles long." (page 414).

The other two sites mentioned in the above quote are the Ring of Brodgar and the Stones of Stenness.

A brief visit to the main chamber of Maes Howe should be enough to convince all but the most sceptical of observers that our Neolithic predecessors on these 'Islands of Light' possessed beliefs and an innate spirituality that would put to shame the cynical, materialistic standards that apply in the modern world. The evidence seems to be that people are starting to search for a more spiritual future - perhaps we could do worse than look to the distant past for our inspiration.

Chapter Nine
'Isles Where Good Men Rest.'
J.E.Flecker- 'The Golden Road to Samarkand.'

Situated in the Irish Sea are two islands that epitomise the sacred nature of our ancient landscape - Anglesey and Man. The first was the last bastion of the Druids against the military might of the invading Roman Empire and the second, far out in the Irish Sea, seems to have to have been known about but probably not invaded by the Romans. Accordingly, the Isle of Man (Mona Manannan) and the islands on the west coast of Scotland were probably the last centres of true Goddess worship in the British Isles, along with Ireland itself (although they all eventually fell victim to that later Roman invasion - the Church.). It is significant that the Hebrides still bear the name of the Goddess Brid, or Bridgit, discussed in a previous chapter.

It is proposed to examine in further detail the Isles of Anglesey and Man and to demonstrate their significance within the concept of the sacred landscape of Britain.

Anglesey.
Anglesey, or Ynys Mon, was an important centre

from Mesolithic times onwards. The Druids had one of their great colleges there, one to rival the one at Chartres in France, south of Paris. As such the island was specifically targeted by the Roman army, determined to wipe out the Druidic religion of the Celts, which, they perceived, challenged their domination of the western borders of Europe.

Tacitus, the great Roman historian, described the start of the final Roman attack on the island thus :-

"On the shore stood the opposing army with its dense array of armed warriors, while between the ranks dashed women in black attire like the Furies, with hair dishevelled, waving brands. All around, the Druids, lifting their hands to heaven and pouring forth dreadful imprecations scared our soldiers by the unfamiliar sight
........."

Probably because of its close proximity to the Welsh mainland, Anglesey bears the imprint of successive waves of human occupation. Its surviving monuments date back over five thousand years and many of them are 'multi-layered', such as Bryn Celli-ddu, which still shows evidence of an early henge monument adapted later into the famous chambered tomb. There are also remnants of stone circles and later religious complexes. The Iron Age inhabitants of the island left their mark in the form of stone hut circles on the headland overlooking Holyhead and at Din Llugwy.

So thorough were the Romans in their extirpation of the Druids that there is little evidence of either the Druids or the Celts extant on the island. However there are still traces of Celtic Christianity on the island - the brand of Christianity that spread from

190

Jerusalem to the western fringes of the British Isles, based on the original teachings of Jesus and eventually supplanted by the Roman church espoused by Paul. Examples of this Celtic influence are to be found at Penmon Priory, of which more later.

The two chambered tombs of Bryn Celli-ddu and Barclodiad y Gawres show that the island was inhabited by the same early farming communities that produced similar mounds in Ireland, Brittany, Cornwall, Wales and southern Scotland.

As Dr. Steve Barrow of the National Museums and Galleries of Wales states, in an internet article on the Wales Past website :-

'In all the areas where passage tombs appear, they are built to slightly different designs, but there is sufficient similarity between them all to indicate that the Irish Sea was a thriving highway at the end of the

Stone Age, with communities from Brittany to Scotland sharing both ideas and ways of venerating the dead.'

Tombs of this type were built for about fifteen hundred years from about 3,500 BCE onwards. As well as the circular shape with an access passage to the centre, they also often have kerbstones around the edge and commonly have similar carvings in the form of swirls, spirals and zig-zags (see Chapter Eleven). The Irish Sea connection is further emphasised by the fact that the remains of a chambered grave has been found at Calderstones in Liverpool (see bibliography). The centre chamber and passage are usually lined with large stones, called orthostats, or sometimes dry stone walls.

191

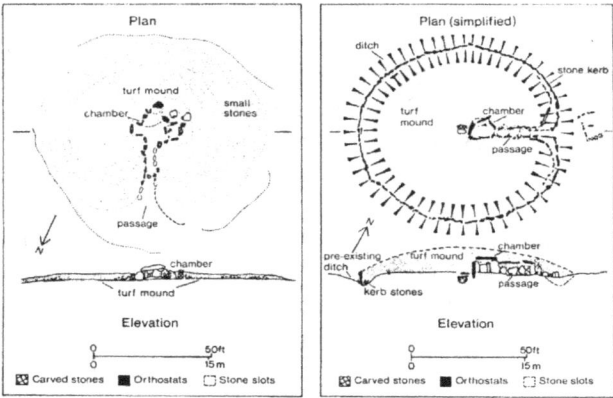

Barclodiad y Gawres Bryn Celli Ddu
Abstracted from 'The Calderstones', after Lynch
(1969).

Some Anglesey Sites (see map on following page).
1) Bryn Celli Ddu (see plan view above).
This is a classic example of a chambered tomb or passage grave (see above) and the name has been translated as 'the mound in a dark grove' or alternatively as 'the mound in the grove of the deity' - these names certainly indicate how the land use has changed in the past five thousand years, as the mound now lies within open pastureland! The tomb was preceded on this site by a henge with a stone circle, surrounded by a bank and ditch. The original henge in all probability dates back five thousand years and now only parts of the ploughed out ditch are visible.

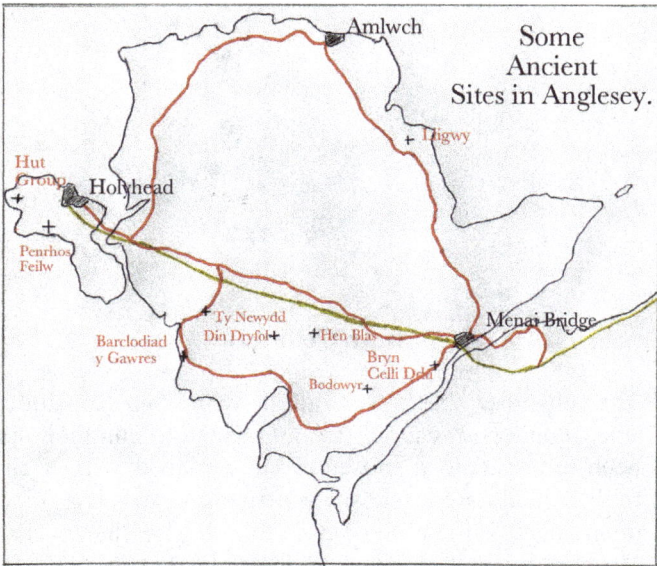

Some
Ancient
Sites in Anglesey.

Amlwch

Lligwy

Hut
Group
Holyhead

Penrhos
Feilw

Ty Newydd
Din Dryfol

Barclodiad
y Gawres

Hen Blas

Menai Bridge

Bryn
Celli Ddu

Bodowyr

The chambered tomb dates back to perhaps 2,500 BCE and consists of a turf mound stretching out to the ditch (see photograph) and a passage facing north east, with a single standing stone remaining in the central 2.4 metre wide chamber. The mound is surrounded by kerbstones, perhaps 'robbed' from the original stone circle, and there are dry stone walls lining the central passage.

Bryn Celli-ddu

The chamber itself is roofed with two capstones.
The wonderful carved stone near the entrance has
been removed to a museum and replaced with a cast
replica. This stone shows a serpentine carving on its
main side, similar to those found elsewhere as at
Newgrange in Ireland. It is possible that this carving
depicts the journey of a man's soul.

Carved Stone at Bryn Celli Ddu

The tomb, perhaps the most perfect in the whole of England and Wales, is overlooked by the gorsedd or 'natural stone of the ancients' (Cope) - a gorsedd now being designated as the site for the bardic chair of the Druids, but in reality dating back to earlier times. The whole natural setting of the tomb, the gorsedd and the menhir, or monolith, of Llandaniel Fab to the N.W., set in the shadow of Snowdonia across the Menai Straits, is awe-inspiring.

As Cope puts it, in 'The Modern Antiquarian' (1998) "Bryn Celli Ddu is a place to stay for a very long time …and marvel at the whole unfolding history of great worship under the stars, the planets, the sun and the moon." (page 306).

2)   Bodowyr.
In modern times, this appears as a setting of standing stones, now known as a dolmen. However the beautiful table shape of three stones supporting a huge capstone is but the remains of an original passage grave, of which the surviving dolmen formed the polygonal central chamber. The atmosphere and energy around the stones is amazing and once again the whole is overlooked by the Snowdon massif away to the S.E..

Cope (1998) claims that Bodowyr can be read as Bod O'Ur and translates as 'the body or existence of Ur' - one of the great goddesses of the Neolithic (see Chapter Two).

3) Barclodiad y Gawres (see previous plan view).
A wonderful chambered tomb on a headland looking westward over the sea - spoiled somewhat by the concrete 'protection' that has been erected over

it. Many stones have been removed from the passageway and the earth covering has been weathered away over the years, revealing the capstone. Once again there are carved stones visible in the passageway. The wonderful setting and sense of the sacred make this place atmospheric, despite the concrete!

4) Ty Newydd.

Another chambered tomb in which all the earth has been weathered away to reveal the dolmen at its centre - in this case four standing stones and a huge capstone. This latter is sadly broken and poorly renovated. Cope describes it as 'a place of sad genius'. However, it retains its 'genius loci' as Devereux puts it.

5) Lligwy and Din Lligwy.

These two sites from different periods are within half a mile of each other and, combined with the old chapel in close proximity, show that this place was special to the ancients over a long period. The dolmen at Lligwy is over 4,500 years old and has a huge capstone, perhaps weighing twenty tons, resting on eight short stones. The central space is larger than might be expected as it is dug below the surrounding ground level. Despite occasional difficulty of access (railings) it is a very peaceful and atmospheric spot.

The stone hut circles at Din Lligwy date back about two thousand years and once again the place has a special atmosphere. These are supposedly huts and rectangular workshops for iron but one may get the feeling that the site had a sacred purpose as well.

6) Holy Island.

As the name indicates, Holy Island is the most sacred part of Anglesey and, as the archaeologists would put it, it forms a ritual landscape, gradually being eroded by the urbanisation spreading from Holyhead. Some elements of this sacred landscape are listed below.

Barclodiad y Gawres Chambered Tomb

Ty Newydd Dolmen

Bodowyr Dolmen

Lligwy Dolmen

a/ The Ty Mawr Hut group.

This is located on the slopes of Holyhead Mountain overlooking the sea. They comprise a series of hut circles about four metres in diameter, interspersed with some rectangular structures. The fact that there are the remains of some fifty structures would seem to indicate a large settlement. Much discussion has taken place as to the age of the settlement, from Neolithic to Romano-British. It 'feels' older than Iron Age and it is possible that the village in fact spanned over a thousand years of history.

Scott Peck in his book, 'In Search of Stones' (1995), a 'pilgrimage' around the British Isles, had this to say about Ty Mawr.

"Whoever it had housed, we knew for sure we were standing on hallowed ground. We had discovered, to our satisfaction at least, one reason why this tip of Anglesey was called the Holy Isle. Even though we were being drenched in the driving rain, we were both experiencing the presence of God. And even though we couldn't stay as long as we wished, Lily and I will always remember those hut circles overlooking the sea as one of the most holy places we had ever visited." (pp. 70-71).

It must be stated that, on a group visit to the site, the circles betrayed no evidence of being holy places, impressive as they were as remnants of the previous occupants. This is not to deny that they lie on the flanks of Holyhead Mountain which is undoubtedly hallowed ground.

Ty-Mawr Hut Circle.

b/ Penrhos Feilw.

These are a pair of long, thin monoliths about three metres apart. They are similar in shape, although not in geology, to the stones of Callanish. They are aligned to the N.N.E.and have a wonderful sense of energy and atmosphere. It has been suggested that these were a central setting in a former circle and indeed a ring of energy was detected about three metres out from the stones, but they 'feel' right in their present setting. They seem to fit in perfectly to the natural landscape with the nearby hilly, rock outcrop perhaps an object of veneration by the ancients (cf. the Hurlers and the Cheesewring on Dartmoor).

Penrhos Feilw Stones.

c/ Trefynath.

Cope in 'The Modern Antiquarian' describes this site as 'built on a superb rocky outcrop, probably the first temple of the area'. This structure is different to those on the rest of Anglesey in that, instead of the chambered tombs, here we appear to have the remnants of one of the so-called Severn-Cotswold tombs or long barrows. It has the high entrance and forecourt for ritual practices, a long passageway with side chambers, all in the truncated 'goddess' shape- similar in style in fact to the West Kennet long barrow. In this case, however, the earth has been eroded to such an extent that we are left with just the upstanding rocks and the side chambers are no longer really identifiable as such.

The Isle of Man

The Isle of Man occupies a unique position in the British Isles, both geographically and politically. Not only is it located in the centre of the Irish Sea, a similar distance from Scotland, Ireland, Wales and England, but it is also central within the British Isles in that a circle circumscribed around the British Isles, with Tynwald Hill (see map of the Island) as its central point, reveals that the island is equidistant from Land's End and John o'Groats, and similarly between S.W. Ireland and S.E. England. This has been commented on by a number of authors, notably John Michell and Adrian Cope. Michell has gone so far as to describe the Isle of Man as the 'omphalos', or navel, of the British Isles. The word 'omphalos' means rather more than just the central point, referring also to the idea of a spiritual centre, or birthplace of spirituality, although the actual relevance of this to the island is perhaps open to dispute. However it has been suggested that Man may be a surviving remnant of the lost continent of Atlantis and hence a departure point for the survivors of that apocalypse. Man has also been designated by some authorities as the site of the legendary Isle of Avalon, to which the body of King Arthur was taken following his death in battle. In this claim, of course, it faces competition from the likes of Glastonbury Tor. It is interesting that the God, Manannan (see following paragraph), was said to cloak the island in mists to protect it from enemies and the Isle of Avalon was, likewise, cloaked in mist.

The Isle of Man is also named Mona Manannan or Ellan Vannin and there are still doubts as to the derivation of the name 'Man'. The Romans knew of the island, naming it 'Monapia', but there is no evidence of them landing or settling there. The name is perhaps based on the Irish God, Manannan, ruler of the sea and navigation, leader of the Irish pantheon, known as the Tuatha de Danaan. He was also the father of Lugh. Caesar knew it as Mona, the Irish as Manann, Manaw to the Welsh and Mon to the Icelanders. As previously indicated, the names Mona and Mon have also been ascribed to Anglesey and there are obviously cultural and linguistic links.

A.W. Moore in his book 'A History of the Isle of Man', (Vol.1, p.46, reprinted by Manx National Heritage, 1992) states "Into the origins and meaning of these names, or rather name, since they are all variants of the same word, it is scarcely the province of history to enter, but it may be mentioned that it still remains a problem which does not appear to have been satisfactorily settled."

There is evidence on the island of settlement from the early Neolithic through the Celts and their Druid priests, Celtic Christianity, the Scandinavians and into modern Christian times - the variety of ancient monuments and artefacts reflects this. The worship of the Goddess dates from the early times and Cope believes that goddess worship survived through to the tenth century, indeed Moore (ibid, page 42) believes that :-

"A further confirmation of the presence of non-Aryan (Neolithic)people in Man may also be derived from the survivals among the Manx of the worship of animals, stones, trees and wells, since it seems to be fairly well established that the conditions under which suchsurvivals as these are found 'show that they date from a time prior to the arrival of the Celts' (Gomme, 'Ethnology in Folklore', page 173)."

The usual determination of the later Roman Catholic church to eradicate any evidence of earlier worship is shown in St. Patrick's Chair and King Ory's (Orry's) Grave (see in the following section) and in the fact that the former goddesses, gods, shamans, priests etc. have been reduced by dogma and mockery to the status of 'little people', haunting the woods, glades and bridges of the island, much as has happened in Ireland.

Some Manx Sites. (see map on the following page).

1) Cashtal yn Ard.

This is one of the most atmospheric sites in the Isle of Man. The name translates as 'The Castle of the Heights' and is the remains of a Neolithic tomb dating back over four thousand years. It is one of the finest remnants of a chambered tomb in the British Isles. It is, or rather was, a long barrow some forty metres long. The stones of the forecourt are still very prominent as are the stones lining the former entrance passageway. There are also the clear outlines of five chambers, all of which would have been covered with earth at one time, cf. Waylands Smithy and the West Kennet long barrow.

2) King Ory's Grave.

This is another four thousand plus year old Neolithic tomb named in honour of Ory (or Orry), otherwise known as King Godred of Crovan, a legendary eleventh century king. The tomb therefore bears no relation to him at all, but was presumably renamed to remove it from the realm of the ancient people. It was a conical tomb but the earth has all been eroded away.

Cashtal yn Ard.

King Orry's Grave

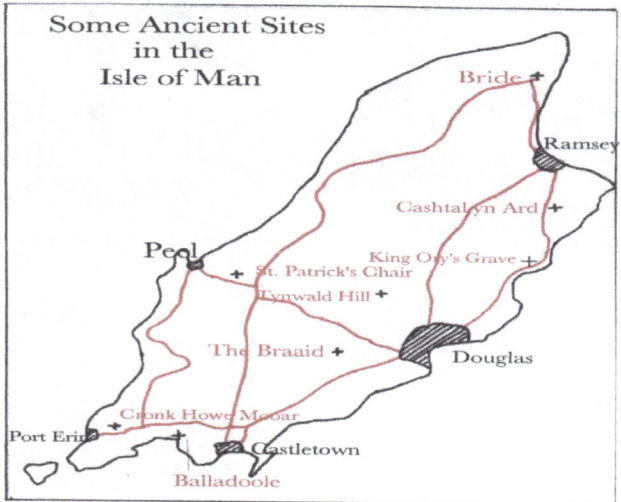

Some Ancient Sites
in the
Isle of Man

Bride

Ramsey

Cashtal yn Ard

King Orry's Grave

Peel

St. Patrick's Chair

Tynwald Hill

The Braaid

Douglas

Cronk Howe Mooar

Port Erin

Castletown

Balladoole

The site is unusual in that it is divided by the main road and part was in a private garden until acquired by the Manx National Heritage. This tomb has three chambers, one of which still contained human remains when excavated.

3) St. Patrick's Chair.
This is alleged to mark the site where the gospel was first preached on the island, by St. Patrick. Be that as it may, there can be no doubt that the monument is considerably older than that. A more likely date would seem to be about 2,500 BCE and the monument seems to be a 'triple goddess' setting of megaliths (see Chapter Two). This suggestion by Cope seems the more likely given the links of the island with goddess worship - see below.

4) The Braaid.
This site has had a complex history which difficult to pick out on the ground. The probable origin here seems to have a stone circle dating from Neolithic times and the name of the site may possibly indicate links with the goddess Bride, whose name occurs in on form or another in many parts of the island. The stone circle was superceded by a Celtic stone roundhouse (16.5 metres across), following settlement by the Celtic peoples. This seems to have been later extended by the addition of two Norse longhouses of Iron Age date, perhaps two thousand years old. The larger of the two 'had curved walls (resembling an upturned boat with ends cut off) made of turf with the ends made of timber. The roof was supported by two rows of posts standing on a large stone. .... The house measured about 20 by 9 metres.' (Isle of Man Guide - internet). The site was large and seems to have been more than just a farmstead.

5) Cronk Howe Mooar.

This is the so-called 'Fairy Hill', which supposedly dates from about two thousand years ago. The suggestion is that this was an artificial hill with a timber fort on the top with a stone-faced motte mound. The mound is about eleven metres high with the remains of a ditch around the base. Notwithstanding the fort, one may wonder if the artificial hill may date back to Neolithic times, as a smaller version of Silbury Hill in Wiltshire. It is interesting to note that 'fairy' is one of the names used to denigrate the memory of the gods and goddesses of the old religion - perhaps the name of the hill is a folk memory of this.

6) Balladoole.

Whilst not as old as the other sites mentioned above, Balladoole was clearly a place seen as sacred by the island's inhabitants. The range of occupation of the site covers from a Bronze Age grave of about 1000 BCE, through early (Celtic) Christian lintel graves to a Viking ship burial from about 900 AD.

St. Patricks Chair

The Braaid

The remains of the boat revealed it to be about 11 metres long and it contained the grave of an important man, along with a considerable amount of

209

grave goods, and also the incomplete remains of a woman with no grave goods. This grave must have been difficult to fit on the hill along with the earlier graves.

Later the Christians built a chapel, or keeill, on the hill, in about 1000 AD, which gave rise to its usual name, Chapel Hill.

7) The Goddess.

There are numerous locations on the island that are clearly linked to the worship of the Goddess (Bridgit). They include Bride in the north of the island, the aforementioned Braaid and Bradda in the south, where Cronk Howe Mooar is located.

As Julian Cope states ('The Modern Antiquarian', page 333) :-

"Bride is a physical outpouring of the Great Goddess perceived by humans in her Bridgit state. All around from Ramsey northwards to Andreas the land is flat and uneventful. As we enter the area of Bride, mound like hills appear and the cleft in the hills carriesthe road to a prehistoric mound which is built so carefully into the general landscape that the mapless pilgrim has no chance of its discovery."

So the landscape around Bride was conceived as being in the likeness of the Goddess, with its rounded hills and valleys (see Chapter Two). There seems no reason to doubt that the worship of the female deity didn't continue well into the first millennium AD. It is also likely in this isolated environment that the Druidic religion survived in fragmented form after the disaster that befell them on Anglesey and also the true Celtic Christianity probably found a safe haven here for longer than in the rest of Britain and Ireland.

Here the, we have two undoubtedly sacred islands that were at the heart of Britain and were centres of the 'old religion' in the same way as Stonehenge, Avebury and Kilmartin Valley, and where the Druidic religion of the celts flourished (to the extent that the Druids had one of their important colleges located on Anglesey) and where the true Celtic Christianity, as derived from the original teachings of Jesus, also took root and survived the Roman Catholic onslaught for longer than elsewhere.

Cronk Howe Mooar

Balladoole

Chapter Ten
A Well of Living Waters.
Song of Solomon.

Spirit of the Spring

"Water is 'other'. Its moods are strange and various. By turns it is quiet, and violent; it can refresh or it can kill. It emerges in a miraculous way from the earth, for it is neither living, nor inanimate; it possesses life, yet is not itself alive and, unlike fire, can never fully be domesticated. Water further comes from below, from darkness, from the place where the dead (in cultures for which that is relevant) are buried, from the brooding presence beneath the feet." (Rattue, page 10).

If we could put ourselves in the place of Neolithic or Bronze Age man, or if these people could have left written records, they might well have echoed the sentiments expressed by Rattue. However it is likely that our ancient ancestors went one stage further and believed that water was animate and ruled over by Goddesses such as Ver (see Chapter 2). Rattue

213

outlines the mystique surrounding water and all its mercurial moods.

These surely lay at the heart of the reverence felt by the 'elder man' for one of the essentials of life. They could see the water descending from the heavens in the form of showers, torrential rain in thunderstorms, even in the mists and they could see it issuing from the ground as the bubbling springs - small wonder that they were impressed! This combined with its life-giving properties made it vital that the Goddess of the source was propitiated.

One can readily understand that the Mesolithic and early Neolithic hunter/gatherers, as they travelled around their territory, must have known every water source and based their camps near them, only moving on when the local hunting became scarce. They would have known which were the reliable springs with fresh water and those which were seasonal or intermittent springs and they would have varied their routes accordingly. It was but a short step for man to view the sources of such a vital substance as being an abode of the Gods. Such places would have been identified by symbols and their location embedded in the memories of tribal or family members - they would become part of the folklore and religion of the group.

As Meaden puts it :-

"In the prehistoric world symbolism provided potent visual imagery to help the believer and worshipper understand the mythology and religion of the tribe, and make sense of the mysteries of life, death and the universe." (Stonehenge, page 49).

As the move towards an agricultural economy gathered momentum throughout the Neolithic period, so the groups found it necessary to develop a more settled existence and farmsteads and eventually villages were established (e.g. Grimspound, see Chapter 2). Here the villagers could build shelters for their animals and walls around their fields in which to grow crops. These sites would invariably be close to a supply of fresh water, for instance Grimspound had a spring located within the enclosing wall.

Throughout all of this time, water undoubtedly became incorporated into the rituals and religion of our ancestors, much as suggested by Rattue (see above). He goes on to suggest :-

"It is easy to see how rivers with their source in caves - ... - could become reverenced, but the feelings accentuated by the cave can be generalised to the earth as a whole, the same images of darkness, origins, down. The link between the aspect of earth as origin or birthplace, and water, is powerfully expressed by the connection in the words 'spring' and 'fountain' in most western European languages." (ibid, page 11).

Meaden (1997, page 25) in his book 'Stonehenge. The Secret of the Solstice', which concentrates predominantly on the female sexual symbolism of rocks, clefts, caves etc. had this to say about springs or underground streams :-

"These were venerated throughout prehistory and well into recorded history, stemming from man's eternal need for water. Recognised as the source of life, the spring and well were held sacred to the Goddess who commanded their powers. Their reverence was continued into modern times, even surviving the prohibitions of Christian doctrine aimed at suppressing them."

We will return to this final comment later.

It appears likely that, in the Neolithic mind, caves, springs and underground water sources came to be regarded as part of the same entity. Caves did undoubtedly possess an overt sexual symbolism as the female representation. Hence the importance of sites such as Newgrange where the 'cave' entrance was penetrated by, in this case, the midwinter sun. Such places would also become involved with fertility rituals - given the male/female agenda and the fact that water was crucial to the support of life. Conversely, caves, springs and wells also became associated with death, as bodies (often as skeletons having been left to rot and be picked over on the surface) or cremation ashes were interred underground. So we can see that a clear link may be established between the 'underworld', as it eventually became known, where the dead went to await resurrection and the source of water - death and life represented in one setting. Underground became a combination of the womb and the tomb. Caves could be used as ritual centres with cave paintings, not common in the British Isles, or symbolism in the form of spirals and lozenges (see Chapter 11), and springs and wells would be places of worship where the water was produced fresh and clear, as if by miraculous intervention, from underground. Offerings were often made at wells and springs to both celebrate and propitiate the Goddess. Valuable items have been discovered in ancient wells dating from the late Neolithic, through Bronze and Iron Ages and into Anglo-Saxon times. So important were these water sources to the ancients that tribal or family groups often left elderly members to be guardians of the spring and to be their intermediary with the Goddess.

Another extremely important aspect of wells and springs, in the context of their place in the sacred landscape, was their value as healing centres, still reflected in places such as Bath and Holywell (North Wales) nowadays. This factor was seen as very important in Roman and Christian times, when many wells and springs were taken over. Clearly the water in wells and springs took on the attributes of the rocks through which it passed - often taking thousands of years in the journey. This mineral charged water was effective in relieving the symptoms of many common ailments. The most common diseases for which different water sources might be effective included eye problems, rickets, polio and whooping cough. Celia Fiennes in 1698 said of the healing powers of St. Winefride's Well in Holywell, North Wales, "they tell of many lamenesses, aches and distempers which are cured by it." Occasionally, skin diseases have been cured by the water taking on a tarry content presumably from flowing through coal layers, which is known to be efficacious for skin complaints. The river Roslin, near Edinburgh, is said to possess this quality. It seems that the majority of wells and springs, including many with a high calcium carbonate content, have the power to alleviate many of the ailments that afflicted children. Other wells brought about relief from aches and pains because they were hot springs and it is also possible that such water assisted with problems of conception, perhaps because of the beneficial, relaxing effect of the heat. When the Roman Catholic church took over many of the wells and springs they were designated as 'miracle' wells (much like Lourdes in France), rather than simply wells where the water was efficacious in

217

some form of healing. As mentioned previously in areas of granitic rocks the water took on some degree of radioactivity and this could be used by the shamans to induce trance states.

As previously mentioned there is a long tradition of people making offerings at wells and springs, indeed to any water feature, dating back for several thousand years. In the first instance, this involved people making offerings in sacrifice to the Goddess of the site. These varied from beautifully crafted flint implements in the Neolithic through bronze and iron to elaborate steel swords and other weaponry - perhaps the grandest such offering was discovered, not at a well or spring, but rather in the river Thames at Battersea. This was a beautifully shaped and beaten shield, totally unsuitable for warfare, but rather for display or ritual purpose (see below). Following from this ritualistic approach to the great wells that provided sustenance to the people, there came the overt realisation that the water might also be used for the healing of ailments, and therefore people started to leave offerings to give thanks for the cures that they had received.

The Battersea Shield

An interesting point about some such donations is found at some wells where people left rags or items of clothing attached to trees around the waterside with the apparent intention of 'leaving' their illness attached to the cloth. As the cloth rotted in the moist atmosphere, so the illness supposedly disappeared. An interesting aside on the whole issue of the leaving of offerings being embedded in the human psyche is the modern habit of throwing coins into wells and springs and making a wish - what could be called the 'three coins in the fountain' syndrome!

It is a sad fact that, as ever, the wells and springs and their attendant Goddess of Neolithic and Bronze Age times were gradually taken over by, firstly, the Celts and then by the Romans and later the Roman Catholics.

Bord and Bord (Ancient Mysteries of Britain, page 156) commented :- "Water was of great importance in the Celtic religion, which was an outdoor religion, and in addition to their sacred groves of trees they had sacred rivers, streams, pools and springs. We have already mentioned the Celtic Head cult and this seems to have had some connection with sacred pools and springs."

These Celtic beliefs were later carried over into the Celtic Christian church with carvings of heads in Celtic churches and may show how the cult of the Green Man came to this country. These beliefs were later adopted by the Knights Templar. The following picture shows the carving of a head,possibly a green man, carved on the elaborate arch leading to the chancel in the Templar church of St. Michael, Garway.

It is interesting to note that there is also a sacred well in the churchyard at Garway. It is clear that the Celts venerated many of the wells and springs that Neolithic and Bronze Age man had visited, dwelt next to and worshipped at in earlier times.

Although Rattue tends to believe that the religious aspect of wells in Roman times has been somewhat over-emphasised, there does seem to have been a significant element of ritual and worship in the pre-Christian religion of the Roman army - most significantly in Mithraism.

As Bord and Bord put it (ibid, page 157) :-

"Water worship was clearly an aspect of Roman religious practices. A number of pagan temples were sited close to water, and sometimes special wells were constructed within the Temple compound."

They particularly cite the example of Coventina's Well in Northumberland where a large number of offerings were discovered, dating back to pre-Roman times, including 'stone and bronze heads and a human skull (possibly relics of a head cult), models of a horse and dog, jewellery, pottery and 14,000 coins (offerings?) and twenty-four altars' (ibid, page 157). The latter were probably placed there for safe keeping in times of danger. The finest example of the Romans taking over and indeed developing a well is at Bath, which has survived in all its magnificent Roman splendour until the present day - as will be discussed shortly.

The Roman Catholic church did its usual comprehensive job of taking over these sacred sites when it came to these Isles. The wells and springs that were still important to the native population were usually 'sanctified' and had a 'new' founding legend ascribed to them, often based on the named saint striking the ground with his/her staff, which duly opened up and provided water or healing for the locals, or by a head being cut off causing the water to flow. Those sites that were deemed less important were ignored and knowledge of them tended to fade with the passage of time. Interestingly the location and visitation of many such wells and springs has been preserved in the minds of the travelling people and gypsies for countless generations.

It is important to recognise that the traditional holy wells and springs remained an integral part of the sacred landscape of these islands from at least Neolithic times through all the successive 'ages' at least until the Reformation in the sixteenth century. It is true to say that, since that time, the Non-Conformists have adopted a policy of actively fulminating against such 'pagan' influences as the wells. Accordingly, within much of England and Wales, knowledge and use of the wells has declined and they tend to survive in their original holy purpose within Roman Catholic areas and those areas of the South-West, Wales and Scotland where remnants of the traditional Celtic Christianity survive. Wells and springs are now largely visited for their historical interest rather than for their sacredness, although many of the so- called 'New Age' groups are actively engaged in endeavouring to reawaken interest in wells as healing and spiritual sanctuaries. It is amusing, yet somehow sad, to note that, in parts of the country, particularly Derbyshire and Staffordshire, well-dressing still forms an integral part of the annual calendar where "by decorating a local spring or well the people would honour the guardian spirit of the water source" (ibid, page 228).

It is proposed to study in brief a number of examples of wells, neglected and otherwise, from the different traditions of well usage.

A Selection of Wells.

1) Starwell, near Biddestone (Wiltshire).

This spring is situated in a lonely rural setting and seems little used these days, save for the cattle. The spring is not signposted. There is an atmosphere at the site, feelings of desolation, loneliness and desertion. The spring was venerated by the Neolithic people in their wanderings and further used by the travelling people over the generations, but there is no indication of its presence now except on the large scale O.S. maps.

The spring emerges as a trickle from the foot of a two metre high clay bank on top of the limestone bedrock. The spring derives its name from the fossil crinoid (sea lily) 'stars' found in the water. There seems to have been a stone container for the spring water at one stage but the spring has now eroded about two metres further back from this. The main energy line runs along the same line as the spring and stream. One can well imagine a small tribe or family group worshipping their goddess of earth and water in such a setting.

2) Malham Cove, in West Yorkshire. There is a photograph on the following page.

This is not particularly recognised as a sacred site but logic dictates it must be. The powerful Vauclusian spring (named after Vaucluse in France) gushes out with tremendous force from the foot of a huge limestone cliff carved by meltwater in the last Ice Age. The impressive grandeur of the setting and the power of the stream emerging from the 'underworld' offer proof that this must have been a holy site. A glance at a map of the area would show there was much ancient settlement in the area surrounding the Cove - making it an ideal focus for worship.

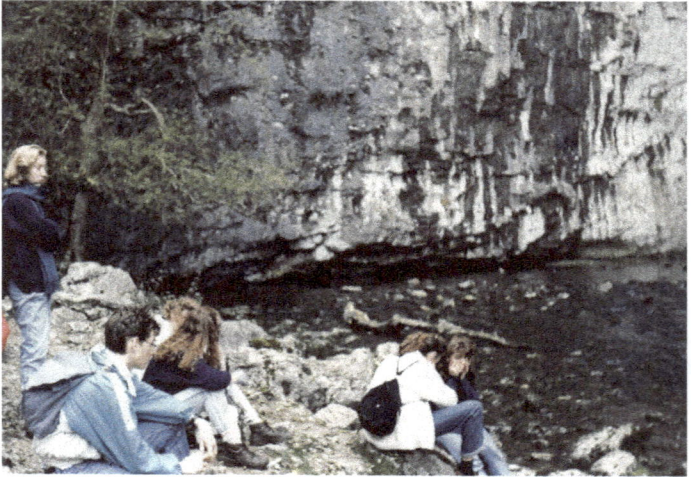

3) St. Nectan's Well, Welcombe, Devon. There is a photograph below.

This is a typical holy well, adopted by the Roman Catholic religion because of the worship of the spring by the local people. St. Nectan was, supposedly, a holy man of the old Celtic Christianity who, when his head was cut off by bandits, put it on the ground and a stream sprang forth. This is a familiar legend when a holy place was being taken over from the 'pagan' religion (cf. St. Winefride's Well). It possibly harks back to the head worship practised by the earlier Celts and their Druid priests and this indicates that the site has been claimed by successive belief systems since our ancient forebears. Nectan seems to be a derivation of 'Nechtan' who was one of the Irish Celtic gods, also known as the Dagda - the 'good' god. It is interesting to note that St. Nectan, apparently facing the onset of the Romanised version of his religion in the fifth century, predicted the return of the 'old religion'!

The well house is reported to date back to the
fourteenth or fifteenth century and is in quite good
condition albeit looking slightly neglected nowadays.
It is very close to the church and the waters were
once used for baptisms. The waters are reputedly

good for healing. Although ascribed to the same saint, this well should not be confused with the one located near Tintagel in Cornwall, which is nowadays the haunt of 'new age' devotees, who leave offerings around the ruined well house and in St. Nectan's glen.

4)   Llangelynin Holy Well, above the Conway valley, N. Wales.

Photograph below.

The old church at Llangelynin is situated in a remote spot high on a ridge near Tal y Fan Mountain, above the river Conway. The church of Saint Gelynin, reputed to dwell here in the 6th century A.D., was constructed at the intersection of no less than five ancient trackways dating back to well before Christian times. They were probably routes followed by Neolithic and Bronze Age people which eventually became drovers' roads. The presence of the well or spring on the top of the ridge was the probable reason for the tracks meeting there and would have been the original reason for the well being venerated. The old church was built in Celtic Christian times as a stopping off place for the drovers and the site would have included an inn and lodgings for the men.

The holy well is located in a quiet corner of the deserted churchyard and is a simple rectangular pool set in a small stone built enclosure with just room to stand and sit around the well. On a fairly typical day, this is a desolate spot with the rain drifting down, but it is possible to picture it in brighter, less rainy times with the drovers' cattle on the surrounding hillsides, and, back beyond that, with the Neolithic families gathered at a good central site for their meetings to worship the Goddess of the site. The water of the well is reputed to be most effective in curing children's ailments. Altogether this is a most atmospheric spot and the church has some interesting details and inscriptions too.

5) St. Winefride's Well, Holywell, Clwyd, N. Wales.

This is one of the last great holy healing wells of Britain. It has been maintained by the Roman Catholics since the seventh century, through all the turbulence of Anglo - Welsh skirmishes on the borders and the persecution of the Catholics during the period of the Reformation.

The Roman Catholics took over the well from the earlier inhabitants and gave it its own legend - that of St. Winefride - who supposedly had her head cut off by the Welsh prince, Caradoc, and a spring apparently spouted forth from where her head landed (cf. again the Celtic head cult?). Her uncle, St. Beuno, a monk, replaced her head so that only a thin line remained to show the junction, and reanimated her. She went on to become a nun and ended up as the abbess of a local nunnery at Gwytherin. It seems that the legend was composed around people who actually lived in the area, as St. Beuno set up a number of small monastic cells in the area to spread the gospel. The submerged rock in the main pool known as St. Beuno's stone is possibly the original focus of worship in pre-Roman Catholic times.

It is noteworthy that both the Cistercians and the Templars had links to the Well, with the monks possessing the well and church from 1240 to 1537and the Templars were appointed to guard pilgrims to the site in the thirteenth century, probably at the instigation of the Cistercians, given the close links between the two organisations.

The well has long been a focus of pilgrimage from all over Britain and Europe and indeed coach parties still travel from London on a weekly basis to partake of the healing waters. The well has survived the loss of its water for a period in 1917 when mining operations led to the diversion of the stream and a nearby source from the same Halkyn Mountain had to be diverted to supply the well again! There is a pile of crutches to be seen in the well house left by believers who have been cured.

The nineteenth century Jesuit poet, G.M.Hopkins, wrote these words about the well :-

"Here to this holy well shall pilgrimages be And not from purple Wales only nor from elmy England, But from beyond seas, Erin, France and Flanders everywhere. Pilgrims,still pilgrims, more pilgrims, still more poor pilgrims. What sights shall be when some that swung, wretches, on crutches Their crutches shall cast from them, on heels of air departing …"

6)   The Great Roman Baths, Bath, Avon. Photograph on the following page.

The old city of Bath (Aquae Sulis was its Roman name which translates as the waters of Sulis). Sulis was one of the great Celtic goddesses and the Romans adopted her as their goddess Minerva. Hence the great baths and adjoining temple were dedicated to Sulis-Minerva.

The Diving Stone, the Great Baths

So one of the great sacred sites of Roman times was also sacred to the Celts and perhaps even earlier. There are also representations of the sun and moon god and goddess (Sol and Luna) within the complex.

Sol

The wonderful complex in Bath is set off by superb Roman architecture and includes three baths as well as the assorted services that wealthy Romans expected of their bathhouses. There were cold plunge pools, tepid baths, warm baths, dry heat rooms as well as the main hot pool where the water rises from about 3km underground at a temperature of 46 C (115 F). The baths also incorporated hypocausts, massage rooms and receptions areas as well as the temple complex and meditation spaces.

The waters of the great baths were credited with impressive healing properties. It is likely that the high calcium carbonate content and heat did in fact provide relief and possible cures for a wide range of muscular and joint ailments. Suffice it to say that the baths have remained in constant use for over two thousand years. The reverence felt for this place by the Romans, and their predecessors and successors, is reflected in the huge numbers of votive offerings left in the waters, mainly in the form of coins, but also including statuary, metal objects and the like.

7) Chalice Well, Glastonbury, Somerset. Photograph below.
Chalice Well is a chalybeate spring, the water contains iron which imparts to it the reddish colour that gives it its alternative names of the 'Red' or 'Blood' Spring. It is situated on the slopes of Chalice Hill on the south side of Glastonbury Tor. Nearby is the 'White' Spring, so called because of its whitish colour derived from the high calcium content, which is now not accessible to the general public.

The use of the name, 'Chalice', indicates a link with the Glastonbury legend of the visit of Joseph of Arimathea bearing the sacred thorn and the chalice containing the blood of Jesus.

232

The Chalice Well spring is known to have been revered by the local inhabitants for thousands of years. It is believed to have been set within a grove of ancient yew trees, sacred symbols of protection since well before Christian times. The well and gardens are situated on the famous Michael/ Mary line, the intertwined lines of earth energy discussed in some detail in Chapter Five. The well therefore derives its healing powers not only from the mineral content of the waters but also from the fact that the waters have been energised.

The Well and the surrounding gardens have become a spiritual Christian centre for reflection and meditation, with a particular emphasis on world peace following the horrific incidents of 9/11, 2001. It had been a place of pilgrimage for thousands of years prior to this and the well head was fitted with its famous 'vesica piscis' cover in 1919, donated by Bligh Bond (see photograph). The gardens are laid out emphasising the 'vesica piscis' design of interlocking circles, a sacred geometry design indicating heaven/earth, spirit/matter, which is a symbol dating back again for thousands of years.

8)   Holy Well, St. Michael's Church, Garway, Herefordshire.
Photograph below.
A quiet and lonely little holy well in a corner of the churchyard of the Templar church of St. Michael. The site has a sacred, spiritual feel to it but it is difficult to find out anything of its history prior to its occupation by the Knights Templar.

9)   St. Seiriol's Well, Anglesey, North Wales.
Photograph below.
This is within the setting of Penmon Priory in the
south-east corner of Anglesey. In the sixth century,
St. Seiriol built his small hermit's hut or cell next
to the spring and started converting and teaching the
local people, baptising them in the pure, clear water.
It is believed that the present well house with its stone
paving and benches is only a couple of hundred years
old and it is unlikely that the stone foundations near the
well house are the remains of St. Seiriol's original
cell. Penmon Priory was erected in the twelfth
century to replace an earlier church, probably tenth
century, destroyed during Viking raids. There are
two Celtic crosses within the surviving buildings

234

dating back to at least the tenth century.

It would seem likely that, given the Neolithic history of the island, the spring had been venerated for a couple of thousand years before St. Seiriol's time.

In concluding this chapter, it is worth bearing in mind the comments of Bord and Bord (ibid, page 158) about the long established belief in wells and springs :-

"But although the wells were now Christianised, and dedicated to Christian saints, the simple people who were accustomed to visit them had no desire to change their old ways, and so they continued to practise rituals whose origins lay deep in prehistory.

They could discern no essential difference between the pagan deities and the Christian saints."

Chapter Eleven
"An Outward and Visible Sign......."
The Symbology of the Sacred Landscape.

From time immemorial, human beings have used symbols to convey ideas. In the time before formalised writing, symbols were perhaps the only way in which man could convey ideas clearly. A symbol can illustrate concepts more precisely than a thousand words can say, to those that are prepared and able to interpret them.

As Tresidder (2003) puts it

"Traditional symbols form a universal language which is becoming more mysterious as we move further away from the thought patterns and world view of those who produced it.

Originally these symbols, typically familiar objects standing for something abstract, such as an idea, quality, emotion, value, aspiration, belief, hope or fear - were anything but mysterious.

Their intention was to provide an instantly recognisable representation, or mental picture, of a concept. Images have always conveyed ideas more swiftly than words, and they predated written words by thousands of years."

From Neolithic times through to the Celts, the symbols portrayed in rock carvings (petroglyphs or rock art as they are sometimes called) are, in themselves, abstract but seem to have been produced to convey ideas. As man has evolved and become more dependent on the written word, so the meaning of the symbols has faded into a distant memory, leaving them to be interpreted by archaeologist/historians or by spiritually minded people who feel linked to the Neolithic 'mindset', or by people combining the two approaches.

As Meaden puts it (ibid, page 49) :-

"In the prehistoric world symbolism provided potent visual imagery to help the believer and worshipper understand the mythology and religion of the tribe, and make sense of the mysteries of life, death and the universe."

Many people have suggested that the distinctive designs found on the megaliths of the sacred sites of Britain are intended for decoration only, 'art for art's sake', however there can be no doubt that they are intended to have symbolic meaning - our ancestors were trying to give a message to those that followed. One indication that the symbols were not intended solely as artwork lies in the fact that the designs were not always left in places that were visible - surely the prime intention of art. An example of this can be seen in that symbols were carved on the reverse, hidden side of some of the kerbstones of places such as Newgrange in the Boyne valley, or hidden away in the dark recesses of caves. Another indication of the purposeful nature of the carvings is that many similar designs are to be found in different parts of the world - the widespread distribution of the spiral would be a case in point here. Neolithic graffiti these symbols most definitely were not!

Castleden (ibid, page 243) seems to distinguish

between some European sites and those in Britain :-

"Most of the artwork that has survived lacks the formality of design, the obviously premeditated composition and the finesse of execution to be seen in the contemporary work of much of mainland Europe. This apparent deficiency may seem strange, because the technology was similar, but the primary intention was not artistic in the modern sense at all but symbolic and religious instead."

It may be worth, at this stage, looking at the religious and social background of life in pre-Christian times. It is difficult to fully understand the life of the ancient people but, strangely enough, astrology may give us some clues. Astrologers have stated that world history can be divided into sections of roughly two thousand years, each governed by a sign of the zodiac, which gives each age or 'Great Month' its salient characteristics. Thus, as is well known, we have just entered the Age of Aquarius which will herald a gradual return to more spiritual values and a softening of the aggressive 'masculine' characteristics by the more caring 'feminine' ones. Due to what is called 'precession', the signs of the zodiac go in reverse order and therefore the sign just completed was the Age of Pisces, with its indecision, change and aggression. In the two thousand years B.C.E., the Age of Aries was a time of aggression and warfare, to some extent ameliorated by the uprising sign of Libra, whereby the wonderful architecture of the Greeks was achieved. Prior to this was the Age of Taurus which included the Neolithic period. Taurus represents permanence, farming, building, grace and beauty, and persistence. It also has, as an opposing sign, Scorpio, which tends to be reflected in an interest in death and the afterlife. Whilst many people cast doubts on the value of astrology in the determination of human affairs, there is no doubt that all these characteristics were reflected in the Neolithic. The abstract symbols of the British Neolithic must refer to those factors that so dominated the minds of our ancestors - how we interpret them is so important.

Poynder (1997) states that interpretation of the symbols is dependent upon spiritual attunement (page 12):-

"The Stone Age sense of inner being is still available to us today; a few people are born with it and some develop it through hard work and inner discipline. It is called clairvoyance and clairaudience - the ability to see 'innerly' through time and space into the hologrammatic expression of past, present and future lateral relationships and events, and to hear an inner voice of the higher connected self in all creations."

Let us look at examples of the important symbols and their place in our sacred landscape. The main symbols of the Neolithic period in the British Isles may be taken to be :-

a/ The spiral - often seen as a double or even triple spiral.
b/ The lozenge or diamond shape. c/ The zig-zag or chevron pattern.
d/ Cup and ring marks - sometimes associated with a ladder.
e/ The sun wheel. f/ The circle.
g/ A serpentine line.
Most of these are illustrated in the following diagram.

239

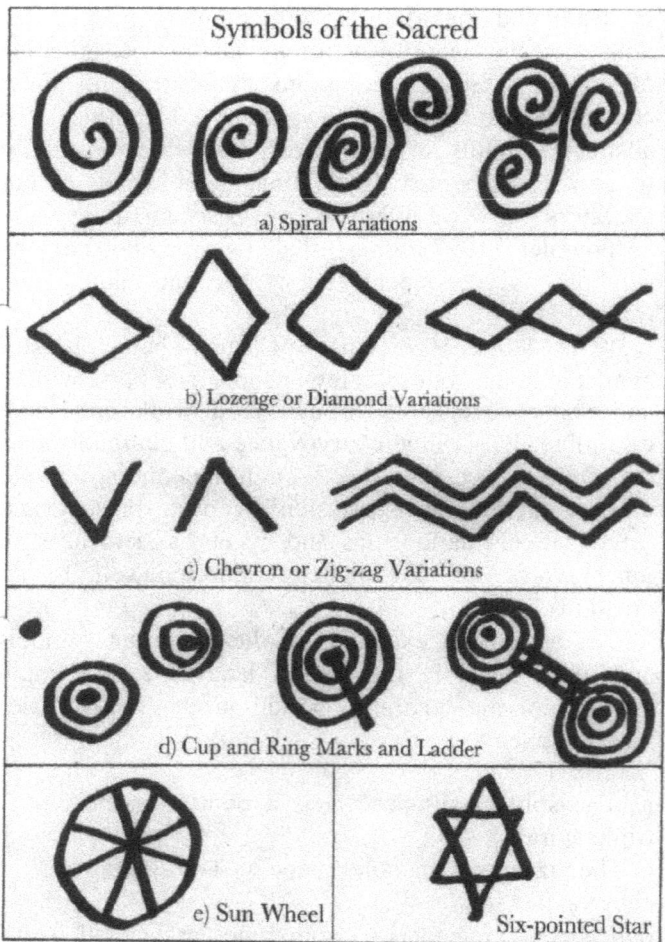

Symbols of the Sacred

a) Spiral Variations

b) Lozenge or Diamond Variations

c) Chevron or Zig-zag Variations

d) Cup and Ring Marks and Ladder

e) Sun Wheel

Six-pointed Star

These are, of course, just patterns carved on to upright rock (megalith) or flat rock surfaces. It must be remembered that the stone circles, avenues and monoliths are in themselves symbols, therefore we have a situation of symbols being carved on symbols.

a/ The spiral.
Jack Tresidder (2000) has this to say about spirals (page 145).
"From the earliest times, the spiral has been a dynamic symbol of life force, cosmic and microcosmic." And "Carved on megaliths, spirals suggest a labyrinthine journey to the afterlife, and *perhaps a return* (my italics)."

Various authors have placed different interpretations on the significance of the spiral, but they are all broadly speaking connected with energy in different forms. For instance, Michael Poynder in 'The Lost Magic of Christianity' links the presence of a single spiral as a marker placed on a megalith to indicate the presence on underground water, what he terms a 'blind spring'. The fact is that, as stated in Chapter Five, the ancients (Stone Age Man or SAM as Poynder terms them) sited their circles on the junction of underground water sources might lend substance to the claim, but we must also take into account the actual purpose of the monuments.

Templewood Spiral.

The spiral at the base of one of the megaliths at the Templewood circle in Argyll could be an indicator of the presence of an underground spring, but there are alternative suggestions (see later).

Other theories have suggested that the right hand spiral may represent the masculine energy, and the left hand spiral the feminine. Others have taken this to the point of the double spiral representing a sexual symbol, uniting male and female. The triple spiral, as seen on the entrance stone at Newgrange (see below) has been seen as a potent aid to meditation. Poynder has commented on the great similarity between the triple spiral in the silent language of Ireland (Ogham or Ogam) and the OM symbol used by the Buddhists as a focus for meditation in the same time period.

The Newgrange Entrance Stone

It has also been said to represent Sun, Earth and Light; at Newgrange in particular it has been said to refer to Sun, Moon and Venus as viewed through the roof box above the lintel; to the Christians it was taken to refer to 'Father, Son and Holy Ghost', perhaps adapted from Father, Mother and divine Light to the earlier people.

A single spiral may also represent the sun (heat and electricity) and the magnetism of the earth. It also bears a strong resemblance to the labyrinth seen in ancient times and perhaps derived from the vortical pattern. It has been said that the labyrinth 'represents an initiation, a symbolic return to the womb, a 'death' leading to rebirth, the discovery of a spiritual centre, the laborious and often perplexing process of self discovery.' (Tresidder, 2000, p. 152). A fine example of the spiral as a labyrinth can be seen at Chartres Cathedral in France, built at the instigation of the Templars in the thirteenth century. It will be remembered that this cathedral and its labyrinth formed part of the journey of initiation taken by pilgrims at this time - a 'process of self discovery' indeed!

In summary therefore, the pairing of two opposing spirals may be said to represent the sacred marriage, known as the hieros gamos to later Christians, the divine joining of male and female for the good of the world (or Jesus and Mary Magdalene as the author Margaret Starbird asserts in 'The Woman with the Alabaster Jar'.) The double spiral seems to be all about the Neolithic recognition of the balance between male and female. It is probable that the male, right handed, spiral represents the sun and the female, left handed, spiral the moon - once again a reference to the Sacred Marriage. It is interesting to note that the spiral is still used today as a sun symbol in some corporate logos. Neolithic man knew about the natural order of things and natural law. He knew that crops depended on sunlight and water. He could 'feel' the energies - from the sun, the moon, the rocks - and he built his circles to focus this energy

244

for the benefit of the soil and the crops. He knew that the balance was crucial and worshipped the Goddess that represented this balance. The spiral was marked on the stones to acknowledge this understanding.

Meaden (1997, page 46) states;-

"The joining of unlike spirals produces a scroll-like coil, as at the Calderstones in Liverpool (see below). It is found on door lintels, rock carvings and standing stones. In it we see a Holy Marriage of the Goddess whose consummation guarantees the fertility of the Earth. It is an artistic statement of the life - generating union of sexual opposites which, by their marriage, keeps the divine cycle in motion."

Incidentally the Calderstones in the park of the same name, whilst they have been moved because of the heavy weathering they have undergone, show a fine variety of carvings on what were the kerbstones of a passage grave. Neolithic man with his reverence for the Goddess in the Age of Taurus had a clear idea of the importance of balance in his world. The male orientated society that came to prevail over the next four thousand years, in the Ages of Aries and Pisces, would have been conceivable to him, as was the tragic imbalance that this produced.

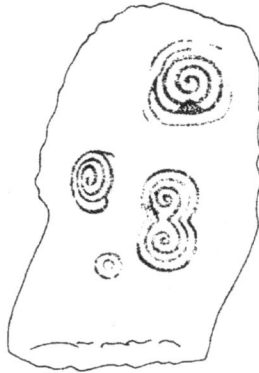

Stone E, Calderstones

Occasionally, to beautiful artistic effect, the ancients seem to have used a fossilised ammonite shell, let into a dry-stone wall, in place of carving a spiral.

An Ammonite Fossil

b/ The Lozenge or Diamond pattern.

Robert Lomas ('Turning the Hiram Key') has commented, based on an article in 'The Times', that the lozenge is the oldest carved symbol known to mankind, having been found inscribed on ochre in a cave in South Africa and dating back to seventy thousand years ago.

As with the spiral, the meaning of the lozenge symbol has been interpreted in different ways by archaeologists and historians. However there can be little doubt that the predominant importance of the lozenge shape with a longer vertical axis is as a feminine symbol. Indeed it occasionally replaces the left hand spiral in this respect as can be seen in the photograph of the entrance stone at Newgrange. The lozenge has been likened to the shape of the female vulva and as such can be taken as a metaphor of the Sacred Marriage, and as such emphasises the importance of the consummation of that marriage for the fertility of the earth and its inhabitants. The shape is found carved on many monuments and megaliths, further stressing this importance. Occasionally however the megalith itself is in the shape of the lozenge. In Chapter Seven we discussed Avebury in some detail. Here the megaliths are both long and thin, male, and lozenge shaped, female. This is illustrated in the following colour photograph. It is important to note in this context that the megaliths represent the woman herself, whereas the lozenge carving would represent the organ. The lower photograph shows the diamond 'woman' shape and has a hollowed out shape on it which may have been

247

taken to represent the vulva. A similar hollow on the Templewood megalith may have been the female symbol next to the male spiral. One of the other female megaliths at Avebury is known in modern times as the 'Vulva Stone' and has a feature on it seemingly showing the vulva with a pair of labia.

All of these examples seem to emphasise, as with the spiral, the importance of Goddess worship in the Neolithic, before the onset of the male-dominated society of later times.

The lozenge has been taken to have represented other ideas in the landscape of the Neolithic. Knight and Lomas in their book, 'Uriel's Machine', have indicated their belief that the eight horizontally oriented lozenges below the roof box of the entrance to Newgrange represent the eight years of the cycle of the star, Venus, which shines along the entrance passage of the tomb twenty-four minutes prior to sunrise on Midwinter's Day every eight years. The lozenges are less clearly seen here as they have been carved in such a way as to appear like a line of St. Andrew's crosses.

Male and Female Stones at Avebury.

The 'Diamond' Female Stone at Avebury.
Note possible 'vulva' shape below centre.

The authors in the same book suggest that the shape of the lozenge also varies with the latitude in which it is located. They claim that the ancients set up poles to measure the angle of the shadow cast by the sun at midsummer and midwinter sunrise and sunset. The readings taken at these times, when extrapolated give rise to a diamond shape. This shape is long vertically in northern latitudes and correspondingly long horizontally nearer the Equator. Lomas, in his latest book, 'Turning the Hiram Key', states that at the latitude of Rosslyn Chapel, the famous Masonic chapel, the lozenge would be in the shape of a square! Notwithstanding the possibility of this interpretation, it seems that other interpretations are more relevant to this discussion.

Marija Gimbutas, in her book 'The Language of the Goddess', traces the development of the lozenge further into a network of lozenges. She describes this net motif as follows - 'the intimacy of the net with the pubic triangle, uterus and egg suggests it symbolises an embryonic substance capable of giving life.... Emphasising the life-giving power of the Goddess.' Lomas sees the likeness of this design in the chequerboard pattern found on the floor of Masonic lodges and the net pattern on the pillars of the Second-Degree Tracing-board, one of the teaching aids used in freemasonry.

c/ The zig-zag or chevron pattern.
The variations on this pattern are shown in the earlier diagram.

The basic downwards pointing V is one of the earliest symbols that has been found anywhere in the world. The V is the standard representation of a woman's pubic area. It has been seen as such on megaliths, in caves and is even used as a symbol in the great art of the Middle Ages, for instance in 'The Sacred Allegory' by Jan Provost (c.1520), where it symbolised the fertility of the Holy Bloodline. The V shape therefore became the cup or chalice of the Holy Grail. The V shape to our Neolithic forebears represented the Goddess that they worshipped and the fertility that they needed for the growth of the crops and the tribal group. The upwards pointing ^ conversely was the male symbol, seen rarely in the rock carvings. In later times the two became combined as the six-pointed star, the Star of David or Pole Star.

The chevron was also seen combined in a long row as a zig-zag. This must have had very different meanings to the sexual symbolism of the single V. Even nowadays the zig-zag is a common symbol for different forms of energy - the horizontal line is a common symbol for waves, water and radio amongst others, and the vertical line is electrical energy in the form of lightning and was adopted as the insignia of the SS in Nazi Germany. It must mean that the zig-zag relates to either solar or earth energy, probably both depending on the context. We have seen earlier that the Neolithic people were sensitive to both forms of energy and set up their stones as receiving centres for the sun's energy and aligned their sites along lines of earth energy. It seems likely that the symbols were placed to acknowledge the marriage between the sun and the earth.

d/ Cup and Ring marks, sometimes associated with

251

a ladder.

Cup and Ring Marks in Kilmartin Glen

Although occasionally found in the southern half of Britain, cup and ring marks are primarily a feature of the northern half the British Isles, mainly the Yorkshire Pennines, central Scotland and at Newgrange in Ireland. The usual setting for the marks is a fairly flat, exposed rock surface, such as the one at Baluachraig in Argyll shown in the photograph above. Usually the surfaces are covered with a profusion of the marks which consist of a cup-shaped hollow perhaps 3 - 5 cm. across and a similar amount deep, surrounded by one or more concentric circles. Occasionally a spiral takes the place of the circles. Very often there is a carved groove running from the cup to the edge of the circles/spiral, although in at least one well known example these grooves are replaced by ladder symbols, this is on the Panorama

Stone on Ilkley Moor. Examples are shown on the sheet of diagrams above. The most unusual example of a cup and ring mark is undoubtedly the so-called Swastika Stone also on Ilkley Moor. Here there are nine cup marks in the form of a X with a single carved groove around and intertwined with them. There is also a single outlying cup connected to the 'swastika' by a sickle shaped groove (see below).

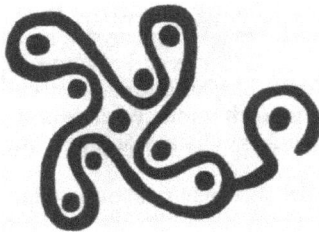

The Swastika Stone

Castleden has this to say about cup and ring marks (ibid, page 251) :-
"It is more likely to be a smaller version of the circle symbol that we can see in the earth and stone circles; as such, it is best seen as a multiple symbol - of the sun, the clan, the world, the territory, the margin from which spiritual journeys might begin."

Meaden, on the other hand, has interpreted the cups as representations of the female vulva, basing this interpretation on a downward pointing triangular sarsen in Wiltshire, which has a suitably placed cup mark in it. Given the sacred, circular shape of the markings, this could well mean that they are a reference to the sacred feminine and the Goddess worship of the Neolithic.

253

However numerous other, more prosaic interpretations have been suggested for cup and ring marks, such as containers for (small) offerings on an altar, a mould, a lamp (oil container) and even as a sort of display case for wares. Someone else has suggested that they represent star systems although they are difficult to relate to the night sky as we see it.

One set of the markings is on the hidden back of one of the Newgrange kerbstones, showing that they are not necessarily for display, prompting Castleden (ibid, page 250) to write :-

"The discovery of a cup and ring on the back of one of the Newgrange kerbstones confirms that the symbol was already part of the metaphysical currency of the Neolithic by 3300 BC."

One might also wonder if the symbols might refer to that other great aspect of spiritual life in the Neolithic, namely ancestor worship. The ancestors were held in great reverence and their bones were often moved around within the territory. It is possible that the collections of symbols on flat surfaces may be a Neolithic family tree, a sort of mnemonic of the ongoing life of the family. The use of the ladder symbol may be a further indication of this.

e/ The Sun Wheel

Royston

This symbol shows the sun in the form of a circle with rays radiating out from the centre like the spokes of a wheel. It must show the realisation by our ancient ancestors of the importance of the sun in the ongoing cycle of life, death and rebirth - both in nature and in human existence.

There are two good examples of this in the passage grave at Dowth in the Boyne Valley in

Ireland. Interestingly enough there is another clear example in the 'cave' at Royston, Hertfordshire, dating back to the Templar occupation of the site in the thirteenth century. (These can be seen in the above photographs). The Roman Catholics again took over this symbol as representing the martyrdom by crucifixion of St. Catherine on the 'Catherine' wheel.

f/ The Circle.

The fundamental shape in the symbology of the Neolithic and Bronze Ages was the circle. Thousands of stone circles and henges were constructed across these islands, as discussed in previous chapters. These were completed at great cost in terms of labour and manpower. It has been estimated (Knight and Lomas, ibid, page 170) that the henge at Brodgar would have taken 100,000 man hours to dig. This henge is cut into the bedrock and is 110 metres in diameter, 10 metres wide and 3.4 metres deep. The circle or close variants of it was clearly of great importance in the life, probably the spiritual life of our ancestors. The circle also played an important part in the carvings of the period - in the spirals, the cup and ring marks and the sun wheel, as described above.

Of the larger circles and henges, Meaden (1997) has written :-

"The perimeter created, at least symbolically, a boundary between the sacred and the secular. The circle was the shape of the distant horizon, beyond which lay another world, chaotic, unknown and potentially unsafe, where strangers lived." (page 47).

This further emphasises the point made by Castleden, quoted earlier in the book, stressing the

256

Neolithic belief in the existence of sacred places in the landscape where people could go to commune with the spirits - the spirits of their ancestors and the gods/goddesses who ruled over their world.

g/ A Serpentine Line.
This symbol has been mentioned previously in Chapter Nine in relation to the carved stone at the entrance to Bryn Celli-ddu. It is found on the occasional megalith and also sometimes in caves. Some interpreters have suggested that they are simply abstract artworks produced whilst the artist was in a hallucinatory trance, however, given the purposeful symbols produced in the Neolithic, it is wiser to assume that the meandering carvings represent something meaningful.

It has been suggested that the line might be a representation of a snake which, given its ability to shed its skin, has come to be associated with birth and rebirth. Whilst this is a spiritually tempting interpretation, one would assume that the Neolithic artist might produce a more realistic looking snake!

It is more likely that the shaman, whilst in a trance, marked out the line of a spiritual journey and this could be later incised into the rock. These symbols are prominently located and clearly held a great meaning to the people. Castleden sees that the link with the spiral at Bryn Celli-ddu supports such an assumption, given the meaning of the spiral.

Whilst many people, including Castleden, have stated that many of the scratchings on the rocks are records of day-to-day events such as farming, it seems safe to presume that the main symbols, both macrocosmic (circles and stones) and microcosmic

(individual marks), are related to the spiritual life of the people of the time - the worship of the Goddess, the ancestors, the cycle of life, death and rebirth.
"---------- of an inward and invisible grace."
Book of Common Prayer.

Section Two
The Message of the Stones

Chapter Twelve
There has Past Away a Glory From the Earth.
Wordsworth, Ode - Intimations of Immortality (ii)

It is clear from Section One of this work that our ancient forebears left considerable evidence of their beliefs and much that can be deduced. They are revealed as being considerably more advanced than historians and archaeologists would have had us believe, at least until recently. Their belief systems seem to have been well formed and their capacity to observe plus their mechanical expertise were the equal of much that has been achieved in fairly modern times. What then is the message that the ancients have left us in their stones and other edifices?

The expression 'landscape' is a fairly specific term covering all the natural features of the land surface - including mountains, hills, valleys, rivers, streams, lakes, springs, as well as the cliffs, beaches, estuaries etc that make up our coastline. It may also be taken to include the natural earth energies that run in lines across our countryside. Therefore Britain's sacred landscape may be interpreted as how our ancient ancestors took the natural landscape and came to understand and use it in the light of their own beliefs and experiences. In some cases they enhanced it using natural materials such as the stone they used in their burial mounds, stone circles and standing stones; in others they modified it by chipping away a stone here or there or adding stones landscape features as at the Cheesewring in Cornwall. At other times they looked at the landscape and pictured it as representing their gods or goddesses, or as part of the female body (a symbol of the respect in which females were held) - examples of these would be Cailleach na Mointeach on Lewis and Mam Tor in Derbyshire. The names given to these features have continued down to the present day.

It is possible to look at our sacred landscape and perceive, albeit tentatively, some development in the belief systems of the ancients in the four or five thousand years leading up to the Christian era. In the first instance, the beliefs seem to be based on smaller, local features reflecting the comparatively small amount of territory that each family, or tribal, group occupied. Thus a cave or spring may become sacred to a group - a place to which they returned on a regular basis. Here they would offer thanks for the fresh water or shelter that the site offered and eventually they would make small offerings at the site and then perhaps an elderly, 'wise' member of the group would be left as guardian of the place. In this way would the sense of sacredness develop (the 'genius loci') and the site may have become specific to one of their god(desse)s. This development was dealt with in greater detail in Chapter 2. The evidence seems to indicate that women played a far more significant role in the tribe or family than was to be the case in later times. Many of the 'gods' in the

261

Neolithic pantheon were female and, as demonstrated earlier, these names still exist in the landscape features of Britain, as well as in numerous place names of towns and villages - the goddess Brid is particularly important in this respect, so much so that she was later subsumed into the list of Roman Catholic saints, as St. Bridgit Many words in the English language may be traced back to their Neolithic goddess origins - this too is dealt with in greater detail in Chapter 2. The early chapters of this book bear witness to the fact that the ancient sites of Britain date from a more spiritual time, a sort of 'Golden Age' - an age when women were revered, with the worship of the Goddess in her triple aspect of maiden, mother and old wise woman (crone or hag). This is probably best illustrated in the wonderful stone circle known as Cnoc Fillibhear bheag or Callanish III on the Isle of Lewis. At this location four stones stand within the circle, a triangular white one symbolising the maiden, the red one symbolising the mother and a black one the crone, the wise old woman. This triple goddess is accompanied by her male consort (as described by Ron and Margaret Curtis in their useful pamphlet, 'Callanish Stones, Moon and Sacred Landscape - 1990, reprinted in 1994 and 2006.

It is probably safe to assume on this basis that women were usually the shamans of their tribe or family and as such would be relied upon to contact the spirits of the ancestors. They were perceived as the 'fountain of wisdom' for their group. However, from about 2000

B.C.E. and the dawning of the Age of Aries, there was a transition to a more male dominated society with a focus on the more masculine traits of aggression, competitiveness and anger taking over from the more caring, compassionate, feminine side. Some evidence of earlier times is illustrated by the fact that a number of tribes were led by women nearly into Roman times, and Queen Boudicca actually took over the fight against the Roman invaders following the death of her husband.

Sacred sites such as the aforementioned Cnoc Fillibhear bheag with its triple goddess setting and male stone within the circle, the constant theme of male and female stones alternating as found at Avebury and the recent suggestion that the huge trilithons at Stonehenge represent male/female would seem to point to the importance of the so-called sacred marriage, the hieros gamos. This is seen elsewhere in the Isis/Osiris story, Ishtar and Tammuz, Solomon and Sheba, and, lastly, Jesus and Mary Magdalene (elucidated so clearly in the bravely written works of the Roman Catholic Margaret Starbird - particularly in her book 'The Woman with the Alabaster Jar'.). It is the breakdown of this hieros gamos that has blighted world history for four thousand years. The sacred marriage is the ultimate symbol of balance in the progress of the world, and this balance has been ruptured during all that time by the decline in the influence of women. The most recent major example of this rupture has been the denial of the place of Mary Magdalene next to Jesus by the Church established by Peter and Paul. In all world religions the place of women is seen as subservient to man. This has helped to create the sterile wasteland of materialism and friction between races and religions, highlighted by Malcolm Godwin

263

in his book, 'The Holy Grail' (Bloomsbury Publishers and B.C.A., 1994). The wasteland is discussed in greater detail in Chapter 13.

Water must have been an awe-inspiring element to the Neolithic peoples. It was obviously needed for personal survival and the falling rain must have appeared to be a gift from the Gods. It could be seen running down the hillsides into the rivers, streams and lakes and on into the seas. Equally, it could be seen emerging from underground as springs and wells - from the Underworld!! They would also have realised that water was vital for the survival of animals and the growth of crops.

Water moves and flows, it shines and glistens, it is cleansing and purifying. It is mystical and is symbolic of spirit. Small wonder then that the springs became the focal point of worship, originally for their sense of peace and later as the residences of gods and goddesses. This reverence was then extended to the wells that were often sunk to provide water. Later must have come the realisation that the springs in some locations provided a source of healing for various ailments such as rheumatism and arthritis, and often for other maladies such as eye infections. This healing, of course, depended on the minerals contained in the water. The Roman Catholic church later made use of these powers to propagate the idea of holy wells. It is believed that in some areas the shamans used the radioactivity in the water (particularly in granite areas) to assist them in going into trance. It was also recognised by the ancients that underground streams carried the earth energies from place to place.

The earth energies as evidenced by ley lines

were clearly important to the Neolithic people as there is clear evidence that their main sacred sites were located where two or more ley lines intersected - this is clearly illustrated at Arbor Low in Derbyshire where a large number of ley lines cross. Not only could the shamans detect the energies, perhaps by dowsing, but they could also augment the energies by using solar energy absorbed by the quartz found in a great many stone circles, as at the Duloe circle in Cornwall. They could also, to some extent, direct the energies, as has been revealed by dowsers at sites such as the Rollright Stones in Oxfordshire. It is clear that the stone circles and other features were seen as focal points for their spiritual beliefs and they perhaps represented places where the 'veil' between the land of the living and the land of the dead was at its thinnest and where, therefore, the spirits of the ancestors could be contacted more easily by the shamans. It has been suggested that this is particularly true of locations such as Stonehenge and Avebury - they were literally perceived as 'gateways' between the worlds of the living and spirit.

It seems that death to the ancients was not something to be feared but rather revered. The whole concept of death was clearly important and has been thoroughly explored by researchers such as Frances Pryor in his book, 'Britain B.C.', amongst others. The idea that sites such as Avebury and Stonehenge had what Pryor terms 'domains of the dead' seems to be fairly well established by now. The ancestors were venerated both as spirits and for the wisdom that they could bring to the tribal group through the intercession of the shamans. As such, tombs such as the West Kennet long barrow and

265

Wayland's Smithy were quite clearly not just tombs but places where worship took place and the spirits were consulted. Our ancestors believed in an afterlife, the continuation of life and therefore there must have been some sort of belief in the whole concept of eternity. It is clear from a wide range of sites from Maes Howe in the Orkneys to West Kennet in Wiltshire that bones were separated into groups and perhaps moved from place to place to be venerated by the tribes.

It is the attitude of the ancients to the cosmos that throws potentially a great light on their beliefs. Modern researchers have illustrated beyond any doubt that Neolithic man knew a great deal about the heavens and the apparent movement of the sun, moon and stars. Evidence from a wide variety of sites from Stonehenge to Newgrange and Callanish demonstrates quite clearly that they knew about the solstices, equinoxes, moonset, the 18.6 year cycles of the moon and the movement of Venus. Clearly the shaman/priests were the ones who possessed the knowledge to measure the various movements and alignments and one can only imagine the purposes to which these were put.

One common assumption has been that midwinter sunrise and sunset were very important because they signalled the turn of the year - after this the hours of daylight gradually lengthened, evidence that the cycle of life was continuing. However so many alignments to the sun, moon and stars have been discovered that a far deeper philosophy must have been envisaged. It seems likely that these alignments were used to determine the timing of certain rituals and ceremonies. The Moon and Venus are clear references to feminine deities, as has been evidenced in other countries and times and probably relate to the idea of the eternal feminine. The Sun and Moon were seen as male and female respectively - the hieros gamos, the sacred marriage. Some of the alignments as through the 'roof box' at Newgrange and at locations such as West Kennet long barrow indicate a link to rituals associated with the worship of the ancestors at particular times of the year. Similarly, Pryor's work in the Avebury area seems to indicate that the great circles were seen as a meeting point between the living and the dead and many cosmic alignments have been identified here.

The ancients clearly felt the need, as has continued throughout all the ensuing centuries, to gather in larger groups at certain important times of the year. Indeed the ancients may be said to have set the trend with such gatherings. However the worship seems likely to have been associated with important times such as the solstices, the equinoxes, harvest time and the associated 'gods' that they worshipped. It was in later times with the worship of figures such as Mithras and Jesus that the concept of the celebration of both birth and death was brought in, particularly by the Roman Catholic church - who set their dates for such 'celebrations' to coincide with the 'pagan' rituals that they were attempting to replace.

In order to facilitate this larger-scale worship, Neolithic man (and his Bronze Age successors) erected their religious complexes in the more populous areas of the country, rather like modern day cathedrals. These can be identified as Avebury, Stonehenge, Arbor Low, Bryn Celli-ddu, Shap Fell (now largely destroyed), the Swale-Ure plateau in Yorkshire,

Kilmartin Glen, the Callanish area, and the Ring of Brodgar - Stones of Stenness complex. Many of these have been described in far greater detail earlier in this book, but they also share a number of features that point to the significance of the beliefs of the people. They all have stone circles or focal point for the gatherings (these had often been preceded by a henge, which served a similar purpose), burial mounds or long barrows and processional ways. Again we see the clear link between the living and the dead in the worship!

In all the religions of the world, symbolism plays a significant role and indeed many signs and symbols have acquired universal recognition through hundreds of years of usage - obvious examples would include the Christian cross and the crescent moon of Islam. However the symbols commonly found in prehistoric times are far more enigmatic, more so in that they were the first symbols to be used and there is no common point of reference to compare them with. We are left with the dangers of interpreting them and traditionally archaeologists have tended to avoid commenting on them, except in the broadest outlines. However many modern researchers are starting to go with their impressions and this is slowly opening up the world of prehistoric signs and symbols to the modern mind.

It should be remembered that writing did not exist at that time, just hieroglyphs (as in Egypt), symbols (or pictograms) and (rarely in Britain) pictures. The significance of symbols is emphasised by the degree of uniformity across the whole of Britain and Ireland. Spirals, for instance, are found from Wiltshire to the Orkneys and from Yorkshire to Newgrange in Eire.

This would seem to indicate that they must have meaning, that our prehistoric ancestors must have thought at least in broad terms about spiritual matters and perhaps about the cosmos. It is highly unlikely that they were going to take the trouble to laboriously chip out a spiral on a hard rock to indicate some mundane issue. The far-reaching nature of the symbols illustrates the point that people travelled far more extensively than had been previously thought - recent evidence from Kilmartin Glen points to travellers from Scandinavia having settled in the area and evidence from elsewhere shows that Scandinavians settled in the Orkneys and people from the Continent settled in southern Britain. It has been shown that there was a trade in stone axes between Cumbria, at the Castlerigg stone circle, and Ireland. Stone circles in the hills above Penmaenmawr in north Wales also indicate trade between that area and Ireland.

Suggestion as to the meanings that can be placed on the various symbols are outlined in Chapter 11, mainly in relation to the relatively small scale symbols found carved in our landscape. More and more of these are being discovered in places such the east Pennines in Yorkshire, Kilmartin Glen in Argyll and at Barclodiad y Gawres in Anglesey.

However it should be remembered that symbols are also macrocosmic in nature. The circle in particular was obviously important to the ancients, given the large number of stone circles that are scattered across the landscape of Britain. The quotation from Rodney Castleden on page 26 of this book gives a clear interpretation of the significance of the circular shape to prehistoric man. A similar suggestion from a different culture altogether shows that the circular shape carries memories from back in time. Black Elk, quoted in the well-known work by Neihardt 'Black Elk Speaks', gives a historical interpretation of the importance of the circle. He was a medicine man (shaman) of the Oglawa Sioux.

On page 50, he is quoted thus :-

"Everything the Power of the World does is done in a circle. The sky is round and I have heard that the earth is round like a ball, and so are all the stars. The wind in its greatest power whirls. Birds make their nests in circles, for theirs is the same religion as ours. The sun comes forth and goes down again in a circle. The moon does the same and both are round. Even the seasons form a great circle in their changing, and always come back to where they were. The life of a man is a circle from childhood to childhood. So it is in everything where power moves. Our tepees were round like the nests of birds, and these were always set in a circle, the nation's hoop, a nest of many nests, where the Great Spirit meant for us to hatch our children."

Significantly, in the same section, Black Elk also points out the energy derived from the circle.

"In the old days, when we were a strong and happy people, all our power came to us from the sacred hoop of the nation, and so long as the hoop was unbroken, the people flourished."

There can be no doubt of the significance of the circle to the Neolithic people, with their stone circles, the round tumuli, the round chambered cairns and their round houses. Black Elk links the circle to energy and the circle permits the free movement of the earth energy. In the 'modern' science of feng shui, the

270

circle permits this free movement whereas energy tends to become trapped in the corners of squares - a point that Black Elk emphasised in regard to the round tepees of the native Americans compared to the square houses of the 'white' folk. Manly Hall in his book, 'Lectures in Ancient Philosophy', states that the circle is the symbol for universal force.

It is indisputable that symbols are a powerful reflection of the beliefs of the ancient people and that fragments of their original meanings have filtered down to the present day. The old sacred sites give an indication of the path to true spirituality for 'those with eyes to see' and, as stated previously, provided gateways to 'alternative realities' where our Neolithic ancestors with their shaman/mediums could access the spirit world. Stonehenge, in particular, has long been recognised as a potent access point to the spirit world.

One of the themes running through this book has been an emphasis on the hostility demonstrated by the established churches to the power that the ancient 'pagan' sites exercised on the people of the country. It is noteworthy that this hostility has been at its most significant during the first two thousand years of the Christian era - long after the belief system of the Neolithic people was established. One must question the justification for this hostility. Did it stem in the first instance from the desire of the Roman armies and their commanders to dominate the native population? Did it stem from the ruthless desire of the Roman church to be the sole arbiter on religious issues in the country? Is it not possible that the overlords of the 'universal church' actually feared that the belief systems of the ancients were in some way more potent than their manufactured religion and based on a firmer spiritual basis?

It remains to be seen how the rise of the Church, the decline in the influence of women and the subsequent rise in aggressiveness and materialism has affected the world during the last two thousand years.

Chapter Thirteen
"Whither is fled the visionary gleam?"
Wordsworth, Ode - Intimations of Immortality (iv)

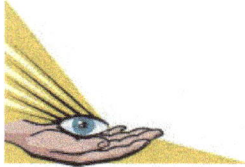

Much has happened to the world in the past four thousand years that has affected the way mankind views material and spiritual matters. It has been a recurring theme throughout this book how the various 'Ages' have affected the way the world has evolved. It has largely become a world dominated by men. Whereas once the tribal rulers of the Neolithic period tended to be female and a matriarchal society dominated - Boudicca, the last great woman leader, although the wife of the ruler of the Iceni people of Norfolk, rose up against the Romans following his death and very nearly defeated the Roman armies sent against her before being defeated and slain in A.D.60. Long before this time, male leaders came to the fore and the 'male' characteristics of intolerance and aggression were established.

A quick scan through the history of Britain during the past four thousand years will reveal the devastating effect that this change has made to our national development. Some of the principal events have been listed to highlight the significance of male domination :-

Maiden Castle, Dorset

1.   The tribal warfare of the late Bronze Age and the Iron Age that resulted in numerous hill forts being constructed exemplified by Maiden Castle in Dorset (see accompanying photograph showing the amazing ramparts and ditches) and Foel Fenlli in the Clwyd Range of North Wales.

2.   The Roman invasions and crushing of the native population.

3.   The so-called 'Dark Ages' with the Viking / Anglo-Saxon invasions.

4.   The Norman invasion of 1066 and the ongoing clashes between Norman and Saxon.

5.   The introduction of feudalism with the great divide between the few rich and numerous poor and an emphasis on male dominance.

6.   Edward I and his dominance of the Welsh and the Scots and the construction of huge castles such as Caernarvon and Conway - although, in fairness, he never totally put down the Scottish (male) nobles.

7.   The British involvement in the Crusades of the twelfth and thirteenth centuries.

8.   Wars with France and Spain.
9.   The English Civil War.
10. The war against France and the American colonists.
11. The building of the Empire.
12. The Industrial Age and the growth of materialism.
13. The Irish troubles throughout the nineteenth and twentieth centuries - a classic case of greed and aggression.
14. The tragic twentieth century with its two great World Wars, Korea and the Middle East, amongst others!
15. The twenty-first century and our links to the world's trouble spots.

Clearly a number of these periods overlap one another but one can gain the general impression of aggression and turmoil from this bloody dossier - granted that some of the events listed were a result of defensive action or in the defence of oppressed peoples. However the overwhelming impression is one of the dichotomy between rich/poor and, almost incidentally, male /female.

Another way of looking at the devastation that man has wrought on the earth during the past four thousand years is to consider the uses to which man has put the bounty that the earth has given to him :-

Man was given fire for warmth and for cooking - and used it for destructive purposes.

Man was given flint for tools, for arrowheads and knives to aid in his hunting and for axes to cut down trees for his dwellings - and ended up using it for aggressive purposes against others.

Man was given bronze, iron and, finally, steel for agricultural tools and machinery - and ended up using these metals for swords and other weapons, shields and finally for guns, rifles etcetera.

Man was given explosives for blasting and mining - and ended up using it in cannons and, latterly, bombs.

Man was given nuclear energy for power and for peaceful uses - and we all know what happened to that!

It is, I believe, of interest to note from a study of the above two lists, of the aggressive history of the past four thousand years and the misuse of nature's gifts that the human race has received, that MAN (as in male) has taken by far the most predominant role and WOMAN has been kept firmly in the background - a situation significantly different to that which was the case in Neolithic times. The predominant leaders during this period came from the Church and from the kings and lords of the various regions and countries, with the Church losing some of its power nearly five hundred years ago, with the gap being taken up increasingly by our political masters.

By the twelfth century this dichotomy between the great mass of the poor and the relatively tiny group of wealthy, privileged people had become so pronounced that life had become a continuous struggle for the great majority. Jack Whyte in his 'author's notes' for his novel about the Templars, 'Knights of the Black and White', stated :-

'Even more difficult for modern people to grasp is the idea that there was no middle class in medieval Europe and only one, all powerful, Church. There was no capacity for religious protest and no Protestants. Martin Luther would not be born for hundreds of years. There were only two kinds of people in

Christendom: the haves and the have- nots (some things never change), otherwise known as aristocrats and commoners, and both were male because *women had no rights and no identity in the world of Medieval Christianity"* (author's italics). It is fair to say that the privileged class was itself divided into two groups - the aristocracy and the priesthood. This is a significant distinction in that, broadly speaking, education was restricted to the priesthood. The gentry tended to focus on the courtly pursuits of hunting, jousting etc and weren't, with honourable exceptions, interested in reading and writing. The priests were educated and education equalled power. It was the priests who selected the canon of writings that were to be included in the New Testament of the Church of Peter and Paul and the teachings bore little resemblance to those originally promulgated by Jesus. The Pope and his group of cardinals produced the doctrines espoused by the Church and it was the priests who read them and interpreted them to the populace. The fact that the writings were only produced in Latin was another obvious barrier to their understanding by the people.

It was against this background that the Knights Templar were established and rapidly became a force to be reckoned with in the medieval world. It is accepted by many historians these days that the powerful nobles that were behind the Knights were the descendants of the Levite priests of the time of Jesus, forced to flee their homeland by the persecution of the Roman armies under Titus in the A.D, 60s and settle in western Europe. These families had maintained their cohesiveness by intermarrying amongst themselves over the intervening thousand

277

years. In private they maintained their Jewish religion based on the true teachings of Jesus, whilst in public they supported the Roman Catholic religion. They sought the re-establishment of their religion which appears in many ways to have been similar to the worship of the Neolithic people - with its emphasis on the spirits of the ancestors, the inclusiveness of their worship and the full involvement of women (as evidenced by the pre-eminence of Mary Magdalene in the true Church). The Knights, whilst nominally part of of the established Church of Rome, faced a constant struggle to move forward their cause and, as a overt force for good, they were wiped out at the beginning of the fourteenth century and driven underground. The struggle to maintain the true teachings of Jesus over the centuries will be detailed in a companion volume to this. The moral turpitude of the Church of Peter and Paul and the out-and-out materialism of the bulk of the lords of Europe was the degeneration of society into what became known as 'the Wasteland'. In the thirteenth century, the first of the so-called Grail romances were composed by people such as Christian de Troyes and Wolfram von Eschenbach, working usually in the courts of Templar nobles. The concept of the Grail incorporated a number of fairly standard ideas in the plot. Ean and Deike Begg in their book 'In Search of the Holy Grail'
(pages ix - x) summarise the legends thus :-

"1. Something has gone wrong. The world has run out of meaning and it is women who first sense this. The old king, standing for the established order, is impotent and the land is waste.

2. A youthful hero, typically an orphan (or the son of a widow - author's note), is destined to find the Grail, heal the king and take his place. Two or three other chosen ones may share his visions and his quest. The Grail is glimpsed and then lost because a vital question has not been asked. This may be a failure of compassion in which the hero neglects to ask the old king what he is suffering; or it may be failure of understanding what the grail is for and whom it serves.

3. The Grail itself is active: something is operating in human lives that transcends conscious intentions. It names those who are its servants and leads them on their individual quest.

4. There is a fellowship or family of the Grail who continue to further and protect its interests in the world."

The Holy Grail, be it seen as a chalice, cup, spear or stone, was an allegory for a spiritual quest for personal salvation. The knights depicted in the Grail stories, although ostensibly searching for e.g. the cup in which Jesus's blood was caught when he was hanging from the cross, were really on a spiritual journey to redeem themselves and to rid the world of the Wasteland. It is significant that it is the women that realise that the Wasteland exists and can help to direct the search. There is also a group of knights, generally recognised as the Templars, who are seen as the protectors of the Grail. Thus the stories hark back to the time of Jesus - the Templars existing to protect the original, true, teachings of Jesus - and also incidentally to the beliefs of the Egyptians and, I would submit, to the Neolithic people of Britain.

Malcolm Godwin, in his book 'The Holy Grail', outlines clearly the dual nature of the Wasteland. On the one hand we have the landscape of Britain and Europe scarred by four thousand years of aggression and wars, and on the other we have, as Godwin puts it :-

"The symbolic Wasteland, on the other hand, was far more pernicious. This was the landscape of spiritual death, in which religious concepts had become so divorced from the feelings and real life experiences." (p.214)

The eradication of this spiritual Wasteland could eventually lead to the improvement of the physical wasteland. However, despite the hundreds of years since the Grail stories were produced with their prescription of the personal quest, Godwin felt impelled to write :-

"Of all known centuries the twentieth has witnessed the most extreme manifestation of the Wasteland. And each of us carries the deadly, self-replicating virus which created it. Each of us carries a microcosm of the Wasteland in the form of conditioning and programming. The Grail legend indicates a way of breaking through that program. The heroic act today, of giving up our lives for something bigger than ourselves, is the only way back to the Spirit." (ibid, p.241)

Has the twenty first century thus far been any better?

T.S.Eliot, writing in 1922, produced a work entitled 'The Wasteland'. On the literary website, Bartleby.com, 'The Wasteland' is described as

"Perhaps Eliot's most famous work, this controversial poem details the journey of the human soul searching for redemption." It includes lines such as the following:-

"Under the brown fog of a winter dawn
A crowd flowed over London Bridge, so many I had not thought death had undone so many. Sighs, short and infrequent were exhaled And each man fixed his eyes before his feet."

(lines 61 - 65)

Much of the poem exudes this air of despair and searching that affected Europe following the first Great War.

To summarise then, the rejection of the influence of women in the day-to-day affairs of the world and its spiritual tempo, plus the sudden increase in the power of men with their aggressive tendencies, has led to a western world in which religions predominate (led, of course, by men!) and materialism is rife. It may be claimed that the world financial collapse of 2008 was triggered by the aggression, greed and materialism of the, largely male, banking sector. This deterioration has occurred in the four thousand years since the end of the Neolithic period. Some groups have over the centuries attempted to carry forward the more spiritual, feminine influence with the hope that, in better times, the pendulum may swing towards a more balanced approach. It may be that that period is about to start.

Despite the cynicism of a great many people, it seems that 'the dawning of the 'Age of Aquarius' has an extremely significant role to play in the future of our world. We are at the onset of a new period in world history with tremendous changes in climate (which may or may not be caused by global warming!) caused by man's callous indifference to natural law, seismic upheavals such as those that caused the Asian tsunami of December, 2004, the great earthquake on the Indian sub-continent in 2005 and more recently in China, and the huge number of conflicts across the world in Africa, the Middle East and Asia. Add to this the gross materialism and self-interest that besets most of the western world and one gains some idea of the problems the world faces. It sometimes seems that we are divided race against race, religion against religion, man against man. These are like a boil that has to be lanced before the human race can rise again and a new Golden Age can commence. People have yet to recognise that the competitiveness and aggression of Man has to be tempered by the more caring approach of Woman before true spiritual values can start coming to the fore.

How can all this be related to our 'green and pleasant land'? It is, I believe, fair to comment that the people of this country, and indeed many others, are suffering from a surfeit of religion and a dearth of true spirituality. As a result of this, people are turning away from the divisive effects of religion and are seeking something more relevant to their lives - something that may be defined as spirituality. Much work still needs to be done before we, as individuals and as a nation, can start moving forward but there are some signs of progress. As the great spirit guide, White Eagle,states in Grace and Ivan Cooke's book 'The Light in Britain' (p.105) :

"Britain would at the present time appear to be

in need of strength and help. Some pessimists may think that her power, her usefulness, is fading. But this is not so. We tell you that within the soul of Britain is a light, a power, which will raise your country again to become a spiritual and moral leader of the whole world, not country with great wealth and possessions, but a country free, ablaze with light."

As more and more people become aware and convinced of the spiritual power that resides in our land and set out on their own spiritual journeys so the light will increase and the example will spread. One of the principal spiritual teachings is that 'thoughts are living things' and indeed these thoughts will be a major factor in the future spiritual progress of this country and the world. It is interesting that thought seems to be a prime factor in the programming of divining rods. It may be said that 'as we think so we are', so clearly sufficient people must change their way of thinking for progress to be made.

We can derive inspiration from our ancient sacred landscape to guide us towards our spiritual rejuvenation. Our ancient sites have suffered at least two thousand years of physical destruction and spiritual desecration by the Church and by unknowing, uncaring mankind. Yet the spark is still there and man can tap into the energy that is stored in the sites built by our forebears.

Knight and Perrott in their 2008 book, 'The Wessex Astrum', reached the conclusion :-

"What is required nowadays, we would suggest, is for people to once again connect with their spiritual roots, to frequent the ancient places once more, to leave the hustle and bustle of everyday life, to walk in quiet solitude up hill and down dale, to truly 'find ourselves. As religions of old have found over the millennia, we need only to *be* rather than *do,* listen rather than speak, experience rather than reason, open our hearts and let our intuition guide us." (pages 258 - 259)

The sheer beauty of our standing stones, circles, long barrows and the like in their wonderful settings can reawaken long dormant feelings within us - they are capable of arousing our true spirituality. However we should not view this landscape simply as tourists with a quick five minutes here and there. Spend time at the sites, don't rush around. Take time to sit and meditate by the stones, allow the energies and feelings to permeate your being. Allow them to 'talk' to you. They will reward you and, in turn, your reawakened energies will help to boost the power of the stones.

It seems appropriate that at the end of this chapter and the book to return to Wordsworth and his Ode - Intimations of Immortality, x.

"Though nothing can bring back the hour
Of splendour in the grass, of glory in the flower; We will grieve not, rather find
Strength in what remains behind; In the primal sympathy
Which having been must ever be; In the soothing thought that springs Out of human suffering;
In the faith that looks through death,   In years that bring the philosophic time."

Appendix A
Some Thoughts on Dowsing

To Dowse :- "to search for hidden water or minerals with a divining rod."
Longman's Concise English Dictionary, 1985, p.414.

Traditionally, the work of a dowser was to search for underground water sources with the aid of a hazel 'twig', but this was extended to the search for minerals using other materials, from hazel twigs, to willow, to copper wire and, nowadays, to sophisticated divining rods.

We would like to think that 'dowsing' can now be achieved in different ways from the above, from the use of the pendulum to the spiritual dowsing that can be felt through the hands, or the effect that some would describe as earth energies effecting, for instance, the pineal gland or 'third eye'. We will discuss this further later.

History

It would seem that 'dowsing' dates back as far as 'civilisation' is recognised at the present time. Nielsen and Polanski (1987) describe how a group of French explorers were working in the Atlas Mountains in Algeria, N. Africa, in 1949, when they discovered four prehistoric cave paintings in the 'Caves of Tassili'. They describe the explorers' experience thus :-

"The final painting was most remarkable since it depicted a dowser, surrounded by his fellow tribes-men, dowsing for water. These historic cave sceneshave been dated by the Carbon 14 process, proving them to be, beyond a doubt, at least 8000 years old!" (p.15)

It is worth noting that the Carbon 14 process has been shown to underestimate the actual age of ancient sites and artefacts.

The full extent of dowsing or divination is now known to have been a world- wide phenomenon. Nielsen and Polanski (1987) again :-

"It seems that dowsing was known everywhere in ancient times. The Egyptians, Hebrews, Scythians, Persians, Medes, Etruscans, Druids, Greeks, Romans, Hindus, Chinese, Polynesians, Peruvians and even (their words!) American Indians used some sort of rod for magical purposes." (p.16)

What is obvious is that the use of the dowsing rod was seen as the prerogative of the shamans or priestly class, both to prevent the perversion of its use and to preserve the sense of mysticism with which it was endowed.

There can be no doubt that the magicians' wands or staffs so beloved of the fantasy writers owe their origins to the divining rods of the past. The great priests of the Egyptians and the Hebrews possessed rods of power that were often shaped like serpents (emblem of wisdom) or said to be able to transform into serpents - as is the case of Aaron's rod as detailed in Exodus.

In Numbers, 20: 10 - 11, we read :-

" And Moses and Aaron gathered the assembly together before the rock, and he said unto them, hear now, ye rebels; shall we bring you water out of this rock? And Moses lifted up his hand and smote the rock with his rod twice; and water came forth abundantly ......"

The important point to make here is that the use of the divining rod appeared as a worldwide phenomenon, perhaps indicating once again that there was one central founding location, such as Atlantis, and its usage was spread from there by travellers across the known world.

As happened with other aspects of the gnosis, or sacred knowledge, the 'magic' was lost following persecution by, firstly, the Roman Catholic church and later by Protestants such as Martin Luther. They actively campaigned against the use of divining rods and, by definition, dowsing, claiming them to be 'black magic' and the work of the Devil or Satan.

However, miners in the latter half of the seventeenth century and onwards were known to use dowsing to discover mineral deposits, and hazel twigs have always been used in the countryside to discover underground water. In modern times, dowsers have been used to discover e.g. underground pipes where the original plans have been lost, and latterly the military have on occasion been trained to 'dowse' for minefields, ammunition dumps etc. using the pendulum. Mediums, such as Uri Geller, have been used for their 'far-sensing' abilities to locate missile sites and similar on other continents - a highly specialised form of dowsing.

Dowsing Sacred Sites
Much has been written in this booklet about the ability of the ancients to locate their religious buildings and monuments on special sacred sites. It is quite clear that the shamans, druids and Celtic priests of the early church used divination to locate their sacred centres in spots where they knew the energies were at their

optimum.

There is evidence that the Celtic priests and the Culdees (pious Irish hermits) could locate highly energised points on which to build their churches and oratories, even where there was no prexisting site - this was no doubt achieved by the powerful combination of divining rods and attunement. This faculty was largely lost by later priests who simply put their buildings on former religious sites to take them over from the 'pagans'.

There were a few unfortunate exceptions to this. For several hundred years it has been the norm to locate churches with no consideration for the sacred energies although folk tales abound of churches having to be relocated following 'divine intervention', e.g. Durham Cathedral and Braunton Church in Devon.

Nowadays, despite the initial hostility of the scientists, it has been gradually recognised that there are forms of energy associated with stone circles, monoliths etc. and that these can be identified by dowsing. The work of Guy Underwood and Tom Graves has been mentioned elsewhere in this booklet. A map of the underground streams around Knowlton Henge by Tom Graves is appended as illustration (see below).

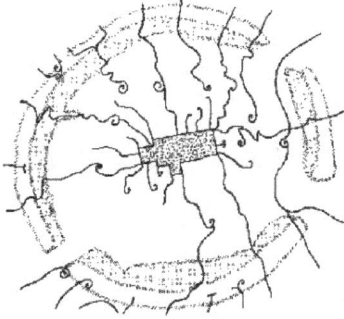

Water Lines at Knowlton Henge.

Dowsers have plotted the the blind springs and other water courses below ground, the energies at the surface around and from the stones and the 'overgrounds' going across country to other monuments. A number of less complex personal experiences are recorded later.

Dowsing

The most accessible form of 'divining rod' to most people comprises two simple lengths of thick copper wire about 12-16 inches (30-42 cms.) long with a further 6 inches (15 cms.) bent at right angles to it to act as a handle. The handles should be fitted with some form of sleeve, which enables easy movement of the rods when held but also precludes the hands guiding the rods.

The rods should be held in front of you, one in each hand, in a comfortable position at about waist height. The tips should be *slightly* below the horizontal to be at their most sensitive (see diagram from Tom Graves book, 'Needles of Stone', below).

The advice offered by Cowan and Silk, 1999, is as follows:-

"Programme your mind to look for energy around the standing stone. We are surrounded by a maelstrom of energies of various types, and it is by tuning one's mind in to a specific form of energy that results can be obtained." (p.15)

Our simple advice is to get to a circle or monolith with your divining rods and focus on energies and see what you get!

Some Personal Experiences

A number of sites have been 'dowsed' either with copper rods with cane sleeves or by 'sitting' on the periphery of the circle.

1/ Castlerigg.
Starting at the edge, a few comparatively weak energy lines were dowsed with rods, just four including the centre. 'Sitting' on one of the stones of the small enclosure registered a strong red colour.

2/ Swinside.
Not dowsed with rods. 'Sitting' on one of the stones gave a strong spinning sensation as if the whole circle was revolving quite quickly. We have since discovered that this experience is often found where the circle of stones is complete or almost so - as if gaps in the circle disrupt the flow of the energy from stone to stone.

3/ Rollright.
Here the rods crossed strongly, seven times including at the periphery, even when moving in from different directions. They crossed an eighth time in the centre, but here they actually spun around as if indicating the primary source of energy. This seemed to indicate that there were concentric circles of energy around the centre.
'Sitting' achieved the spinning sensation as outlined above.

4/ Knowlton Henge.
Here the rods crossed five times when moving from the periphery towards the centre, from different directions. When within about one metre of the ruined Norman church in the centre, the rods twisted away strongly, i.e. pointing outwards as if repelled by the church. No energy was recorded within the ruins. It

will be remembered that churches were often located on ancient sites both to 'take them over' and to block the earth energy flow.

'Sitting' in the church beforehand registered a 'dome' over it.

5/ Mayburgh Henge (Cumbria).
Here the energies were strong, with the rods actually spinning as the energy lines were crossed, seven times on the way to the centre. The centre was several metres from the one remaining stone of the 'four-poster' that had been there, i.e. it would have indicated the centre of the four stones.

Appendix B.
Some Examples of Leys.

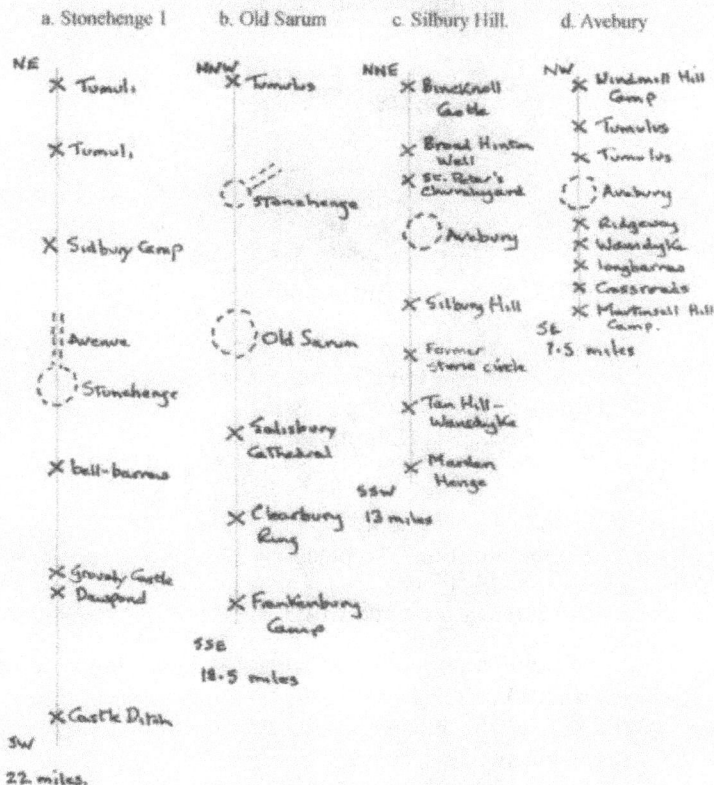

a. Stonehenge 1   b. Old Sarum   c. Silbury Hill.   d. Avebury

a. Stonehenge 1

NE

X Tumuli

X Tumuli

X Sidbury Camp

Avenue

Stonehenge

X bell-barrows

X Grovely Castle
X Dawspond

X Castle Ditch

SW

22 miles.

b. Old Sarum

NNW
X Tumulus

Stonehenge

Old Sarum

X Salisbury Cathedral

X Clearbury Ring   13 miles

X Frankenbury Camp

SSE

18.5 miles

c. Silbury Hill.

NNE
X Knucknoll Castle

X Broad Hinton Well

X St. Peter's Churchyard

Avebury

X Silbury Hill

X Former stone circle

X Tan Hill — Wansdyke

X Marden Henge

SSW

12 miles

d. Avebury

NW
X Windmill Hill Camp

X Tumulus

X Tumulus

Avebury

X Ridgeway
X Wansdyke
X longbarrows
X Crossroads
X Martinsell Hill Camp.

SE

7.5 miles

Based on 'The Ley Hunter's Companion' (Devereux and Thomson) and 'Ley Lines' (Danny Sullivan)

293

Appendix C

Long Meg and Her Daughters.

Reflections.

Whose were the feet in ancient days
That walked these wild, undiscovered ways?
And did they gather at the solstice
To praise their gods of earth and forest?

Their faith and belief were beyond
our scope, To drag granite rocks
down mountain slope. To place the
rocks around the crest
Set so accurately, east and west.

The circle of watchers silent stands Maintaining witness
in northern lands,
While Long Meg herself, the shaman's stone, Inscribed
with magic symbols, stands alone.

Two ancient rowans guard the place, Sacred sentinelsin
sacred space.

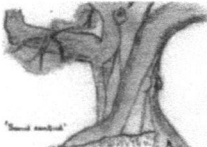

Their gnarled and twisted trunks will
share Their deepest secret with those
who care.

Today we stand on this hallowed ground And feel the
spirits all around.

They gather round to tell their tale
And silently weep lest mankind should fail.

Appendix D

Gustave Dore
'The faintly shadowed track' Lancelot approaches
Astolat Castle,
From Lord Tennyson's poem 'Elaine'.

SACRED LANDSCAPE

Bibliography

1/ Beckett, Michael. 1984 'The Pyramid and the Grail'Lailothen Press.Romsey.

2/ Bord, Colin and Janet. 1982. 'Earth Rites'. Book Club Associates, London.

3/ Burl, Aubrey. 1995.'Stone Circles of Britain, Ireland and Brittany'.Yale U.P.

4/ Butter, R. 1999. 'Kilmartin'. Kilmartin House trust.

5/ Castleden, Rodney. 1990. 'The Stonehenge People'. Routledge, London.

6/ Castleden, R. 2000. 'Ancient British Hill Figures'. S.B. Publications.

7/ Cope, Julian. 1998. 'The Modern Antiquarian'. Thorsons.

8/ Cope, Julian. 2004. 'The Megalithic European' . Elemis.

9/ Cowan, David and Silk, Anne. 1999. 'Ancient Energies of the Earth'.
Thorsons, London.

10/ Cowan and Arnold. 2003. 'Ley Lines and Earth Energies'. Adventures Unlimited Press, Illinois.

11/ Dames, Michael. 1997. 'The Avebury Cycle'. Thomas and Hudson, London

12/ Darvill, Timothy, Stamper, Paul and Timby, Jane. 2002. 'England. An Archaeological Guide'. Oxford U.P.

13/ Devereux, Paul. 1999. 'Places of Power'. Blandford, U.K.

14/ Devereux, Paul. 2001. 'Stone Age Soundtracks'. Vega. London.

15/ Devereux, Paul. 2000. 'The Sacred Place'. Cassell and Co. London.

16/ Devereux, Paul and Thomson, Ian. 1979. 'The Ley Hunter's Companion'.
Thames and Hudson, London.

17/ Ellis, Ralph. 2001.'Thoth. Architect of the Universe'. Edfu Books,Cheshire

18/ Furlong, David. 1997. 'The Keys to the Temple'. Piatkus, London.

19/ Garnham, Trevor. 2004. 'Lines on the Landscape Circles from the Sky'.Tempus Publications, Gloucestershire.

20/ Graves, Tom. 1986. 'Needles of Stone Revisited'. Gothic Image, Glaston.

21/ Hadingham, Evan.1976. 'Circles and Standing Stones'. Anchor Books, N.Y

22/ Havelock Fidler, J. 1983. 'Ley Lines. Their Nature and Properties' . Turnstone Press, Northamptonshire.

23/ Hodgson, Joan. 1978. 'Astrology. The Sacred Science'. Cambridge U.P.

24/ Hoskins, W.G. 1985. 'The Making of the English Landscape'. Penguin.

25/ Ivimy, John. 1974. 'The Sphinx and the Megaliths'. Abacus (Sphere BooksLtd.), London.

26/ Macinnes, L. 1994. 'Anglesey'. CADW.

27/ Mann, Nicholas. 1997. 'The Isle of Avalon'. Llewellyn Worldwide,Minnesota.

28/ Meaden, Terence. 1997. 'Stonehenge. The Secret of the Solstice'. SouvenirPress, London.

29/ Michell, John. 1984. 'A New View Over Atlantis'. Thames and Hudson,London.

30/ Michell, John. 1997. 'New Light on the Ancient Mystery of Glastonbury'.
Gothic Image, Glastonbury.

31/ Michell, John. 1996. 'Sacred England'. Gothic Image, Glastonbury.

32/ Milligan and Burl. 1999. 'Circles of Stone'. Harvell Press, London.

33/ Neihardt, John G. 2000. 'Black Elk Speaks'.

Univ.of Nebraska Press

34/ Newham, C.A. 1993. 'The Astronomical Significance of Stonehenge'. Coates and Parker.

35/ Nielsen and Polanski. 1987. 'Pendulum Power'. Destiny Books, Vermont.

36/ North, John. 1996. 'Neolithic Man and the Cosmos'. Harper Collins, London.

37/ Oken, Alan. 1988. 'Alan Oken's Complete Astrology'. Bantam, London.

38/ Pitts, Mike. 2000. 'Hengeworld'. Arrow Books.

39/ Ponting, G. and M. 1977. 'The Standing Stones of Callanish'. Essprint Ltd., Stornoway.

40/ Poynder, Michael. 1992. 'Pi in the Sky'. The Collins Press, Cork.

41/ Poynder, Michael. 2000. 'The Lost Magic of Christianity'. Green Magic, London.

42/ Pryor, Francis. 2003. 'Britain B.C.'. Harper Perennial.

43/ Rattue, James. 2001. 'The Living Stream'. Boydell Press, Suffolk.

44/ Richardson, Alan. 2001. 'Spirits of the Stones'. Virgin Publishing, London.

45/ Service and Bradbury. 1993. 'The Standing Stones

of Europe' . Dent Ltd., London.

46/ Sullivan, Danny. 1999. 'Ley Lines'. Piatkus, London.

47/ Timpson, John. 2001?. 'Timpson's Ley Lines'. Cassell and Co., London.

48/ Underwood, Guy. 1969. 'The Pattern of the Past'. Museum Press, London.

49/ Young, John . 2003.'Sacred Sites of the Templars'. Four Winds Press, Mass

Sacred Sites in Britain Appendices

Appendix A - A Case Study - The Rudston Monolith.

Appendix B - Some Thoughts on Dowsing.

Appendix C - Long Meg - A Personal View. Appendix

D - The Faintly Shadowed Track.   Appendix E -

Astronomical Alignments at Stonehenge.

www.ingramcontent.com/pod-product-compliance
Lightning Source LLC
Chambersburg PA
CBHW050644270326
41927CB00012B/2875